The English and Sex

Or

The Shadow of Hypocrisy

Richard Goodall

The author is a retired solicitor who lives in Hertfordshire with his first (and only) wife. He has three children and six grandchildren, which might just be enough.

This is not his first work. He has also had published in 1995 "The Comfort of Sin: Prostitutes and Prostitution in the 1990s" (ISBN 1-898823-10-3) where he argues for the full decriminalisation of prostitution and the establishment of licensed, supervised and medically controlled brothels.

He maintains that such a solution, if it doesn't eliminate, would noticeably reduce the amount of violence against women and children and the presence of the sexual excrement on our streets and in our society.

Richard Goodall also had published in 2000 "The Divorce Dilemma" (ISBN 1-898823-45-6), a study of marital incompatibility.

Cover design by Fiona Lonsdale

To my wife

Index

Introduction

Terminology

The description 'the English' in the title and in the book is an elliptical and, indeed, inaccurate formulation. What it means to convey, however, is that the attitudes and the behaviour which are being described are of those people who could be classified as English, (whatever the adjective means) at least negatively, namely that they are not first or second generation immigrants of black, Arab or Mediterranean origin; rather, that they are of a more northern origin.

If it be true, as some recent scientific studies show, that the 'northern' if not Germanic and Scandinavian influence on the English race is possibly less significant than believed, especially since at least two chromosomes found in the English blood are said to originate from north-west Spain... (from the Basque region, in fact), it remains a fact that the Anglo-Saxon influence on the English is fairly substantial. Even if it is not truly genetic, it is definitely cultural and social in origin.

A true Englishman, of course, doesn't exist in the sense that there is no purity for any race (*pace* Hitler and others like him) but the fact remains that the identification in the English of a Germanic influence, despite the blending of cultures generally in our country, is not too difficult to make and is a function of the northerners' invasions of England. Furthermore, starting in the 9th century with the arrival of the Vikings, in the 11th with that of the Normans, and going on to the numerous religious sects of the 16th and 17th centuries, as well as to the influx of the Huguenots, it was inevitable that after the Reformation there would develop in England a kind of Englishness and Anglicanism, which was quite distinctive: and an English culture followed quite naturally.

The Jutes and the Anglo-Saxons mixed over the centuries with the new influxes and, if not absorbed, were certainly affected by the new set-up as well as over the centuries by the plurality of religions.

It has always been one of the merits of the English nation to absorb diversity without too much pain, at least until more recent times (whether we are still succeeding in doing this, however, has now become a moot question).

Hence the description 'English', which is quite embracing though somewhat imprecise.

Note

The "sex" dealt with in this book is principally that between man and woman since its author has no direct experience of other manifestations of the instinct that plays such a big part in human affairs: accordingly, save for some brief, incidental reference, no attempt will be made here to analyse, save possibly to comment, on kinds of sexual behaviour other than the heterosexual, unless the context requires it.

Preface

'Non Angli sed Angeli' (not Angles but Angels), Pope Gregory the Great is alleged to have said in 573, when he first saw in Rome some Angle slaves. Indeed, he was so touched by his vision of the blonde specimens of English manhood that he decided to send Augustine to convert England to Christianity.

And off Augustine went in 595 leading a mission to Britain with the aim of converting the pagan King Aethelberht to Christianity. He left the Rome church of San Gregorio al Celio for England with a group of Benedictine monks. His mission was a great success: it is recorded that at Christmas 597 10,000 Angli were baptised as Christians.

We know a lot about Augustine of Canterbury, as he became known, the first English Archbishop of Italian origin, but there is no evidence that he shared the view of the learned Pope.

The Angles may have looked angelic but perhaps they were anything but… as may become apparent from what follows.

CHAPTER ONE – Lots of Sex, Please: We Are English

The people of the Mediterranean believe that three things should be enjoyed in life: food, sex and art. This may sound crude but is a reality, since you must eat in order to survive and reproduce. The better the food, the more satisfactory the sexual performance; at least, so this argument runs!

Once survival, perpetuation of the species (and related sexual enjoyment) are taken care of, one can stop, reflect and appreciate the finer things in life, thus developing a sense of beauty and artistic appreciation.

It is not here suggested that since we in England often do not eat well, for that reason alone, we the English are not interested in sex. Quite the reverse: the title of the long-running comedy "No Sex Please, We're British" is entirely inappropriate, for it is not true that the English do not think about sex: on the contrary, they are obsessed by it. Such obsession knows no class distinction: the lower, middle and upper classes, and particularly the so-called aristocracy, are equally affected.

One need only spend a little time watching television or reading books, newspapers, or other publications, especially some women's magazines, to discover that matters appertaining to sexual activity are the only subjects which interest viewers and readers and sell copies.

An easy and probably true explanation could be that in England we are swamped by American and feminist “culture”; but the people here are facile prey because, essentially, sexual activity troubles us.

It troubles us because it does not appear to have a satisfactory outcome and, as a result, people don’t understand it, are bothered by it, and are often frightened of it. Feelings such as these cloud judgements and force us into a haven of hypocrisy, which is unsatisfactory for the individual, but more especially for society as a whole because it establishes a pattern of acceptable dissatisfied, unfulfilled behaviour, which in most cases is unrealistic and to compensate for which forms of sexual activity other than the more ‘normal’ ones have to be sought.

What the English, in common with most northern people, fail to remember is that the sexual instinct is a close companion of the survival instinct. Food and sex go hand in hand: you eat to survive and you have sex to reproduce (and to enjoy it as well, of course...). Regardless of national, religious or individual variations on the theme, nothing is more powerful and important than these two fundamental instincts, reactions to which govern individual lives as well as national and, quite often, world history.

(As an aside, it is not easily understood how the English language could possibly have developed the expression "to have sex" which is so divorced from English reality: "to have sex" is so matter of fact, so positive, so much to the point and ultimately, so un-English. There are no truly equivalent expressions in any of the Latin languages; but that is by the by.)

The pains of hunger are assuaged by a good meal after which, theoretically, human beings would prefer to rest. Similarly, the sexual instinct should be satisfied by a good performance. In the same manner as one forgets about food when one's stomach is full, one ought to forget about sex when one's sexual energies have been satisfactorily discharged.

English reality, however, is completely different since very often there is little satisfaction in sexual activity, and that is precisely the reason why the sexual leaning, if not the desire, remains alive, nagging in the psyche. That is what is meant here by the observation that the English are obsessed by sex: it is not that we have too much of it in the physical sense, but rather that what we have is so unsatisfactory that we keep thinking about it and, when we do not, we feel that we have to be reminded of it by pornographic images, or in other less 'natural' forms. Hence the ever-increasing spread of pornography of all kinds to the irreparable damage to our children.

One of the most unfortunate consequences of this preoccupation with sex are the constant, repetitive references to sexual activity we find all around us, usually against the background of smuttiness of the kind much more funnily displayed in the 'Carry On' films (the whole 30 of them), with continuous references to saucy, lavatorial-style behaviour. We cannot say that we have imported them from the USA, since they have been in England for a long time; just think of the traditional seaside-type postcards.

This excessive concern about matters sexual takes a number of rather extreme, twisted and, on the whole, aesthetically objectionable forms; once upon a time, more of a heterosexual kind, now increasingly of a homosexual nature, both male and female. Forms which can often be quite unpleasant, since for most of the time they are, in fact, obscene; perhaps not obscene in the strict legal sense (whatever that sense may mean nowadays, a matter about which there can be extensive debate) but principally in the sense that they are inelegant. Obscenity is, in great part, lack of style. To that extent, our attitude to sex and to matters sexual is obscene because, for whatever reason – whether as a result of our subservience to America, to political correctness, to homosexuality, or to feminism, or whatever else one may wish to think about as affecting our behaviour – elegance of style is something that we no longer pay much attention to in the western world; obviously and more particularly, in England.

This is possibly why we indulge in the frequent use of four letter words and, above all, in "literary" representations of all kinds of sexual behaviour and activity, often in the most graphic and offensive form, as in sex computer games for young children showing scantily-dressed young girls purporting to 'striptease, partner-swapping, girl-on-girl kissing, scenes of sexual intercourse' (never an elegant display) etc. Nor should one forget that our modern young girls tend to dress and to wear clothes which are more suitable for older women. Indeed, very often an observant male may be tempted to consider that the young girl so scantily dressed is in fact a prostitute. It has been said more than once that prostitutes themselves have been known to object to young girls walking about the streets of major cities scantily dressed since they might affect the prostitutes' business...

Of course, it must be conceded that in the majority of cases the type of clothes worn by our young girls may primarily be the result of the current fashion if not an act of rebellion either against their own parents or against society as a whole. The 'rebellious' activity of youngsters is a well-known feature of any society. The trouble is that in earlier times such rebelliousness mellowed and indeed was almost a prerequisite of conformity at more mature ages. Unfortunately, this conversion of rebelliousness into what one ought perhaps to define as maturity doesn't appear to be too significant a feature of modern English society.

This 'fashion' is shared with the Americans and is undoubtedly the result of an unbalanced, unsatisfied, dissatisfied, if not impotent sexual life, especially among writers. Picking at random, D H Lawrence, Norman Mailer, Henry Miller, Kenneth Tynan, all must have had something wrong with their sexual life. Yes, even David Herbert Richards Lawrence, despite the fact that he was very keen to advertise his heterosexuality. What we shall never be able to do is to ask Frieda von Richthofen how good a lover he was; failing that, however, we are entitled to ask why he had any particular need to go into print in such caustic, if not irreverent form, not only in "Lady Chatterley's Lover", but also in his poems and his drawings.

D H Lawrence had his own problems, of course; he was a little too concerned about the importance of what he considered to be the all-pervasiveness of sexuality: his insistence on a "phallic divinity" and his overall dedication to matters sensual rather than spiritual is clearly the mark of a psychological, northern obsession with sexuality that fails to find a satisfactory physical outlet. Fortunately, he was an excellent writer.

The difficulty with the English is that we struggle to distinguish between sensuality and rationality, between the body and the mind, and we attribute disproportionate importance either to the one or to the other without succeeding in acknowledging the need for the two to co-exist. One of our principal difficulties appears to be the inability, which is particularly marked in the case of northern people generally, to understand that in the sexual sphere we can separate physical from mental activity to a fairly considerable extent. Love and lust are not coincident so what is happening is that since there are no official outlets for lust and since of itself lust is not an anti-social activity, we tend to confuse the two (a confusion compounded by the determination of modern woman to perform all roles). One must underline this incapacity, let alone unwillingness, to distinguish between love and lust, the sacred and the profane, a dichotomy which we cannot easily overcome and which may explain, at least in part, our need to escape to the Mediterranean. After all, it cannot be a coincidence that a famous homosexual English writer, E M Forster, stated "the Mediterranean is the norm" (it is doubtful whether this saying is at the forefront of the minds of those innumerable young girls from Scandinavia, Germany, the USA and the UK who flock to Mediterranean countries like Greece, Italy and Spain to enjoy a better kind of attention and practical sexual education than they have at home).

There is a lot to be said for the argument that sexual activity, whether for reproduction or for pleasure, is an intimate, if not religious, expression of two individuals. It requires little public examination and should not be a means to titillate, whether for profit, self aggrandisement or confessional purposes. But the English do not look at the matter in this light. One should add that the surfeit of writing, filming and discussing of sexual aspects in our lives is a feature which is typical of American and northern climes (England, Germany, Scandinavia, and so on) and highlights a basic dissatisfaction with performance. Such surfeit is also spreading fast to Mediterranean countries.

This type of behaviour is unpleasant and contagious. Not too long ago (October 2001) one read about Kenneth Tynan's daughter going into print at considerable length about her father's homosexuality and sado-masochism. One is entitled to ask oneself why she did it. Each of us has, no doubt, different views about reserve and family pride: but the occurrence is symptomatic and unkind to the memory of her father, for she shows no reticence about indicating that he enjoyed sexual activities like the caning of schoolgirls, was a fetishist about underwear, and was not averse to indulging in masturbation.

No comparison, of course, is made nor is it suggested that other populations are better on this score: bad taste permeates the whole of the world, especially the western one. The point, however, is that this is one instance of what has been referred to above as an obsession, which could not and would not be accepted, publicised in writing or on television, where one had a more balanced and open attitude to matters sexual.

It is somewhat trite to say that human beings are all the same whatever their race, creed, nationality and colour. Of course we are. We all have the same needs: to eat, to drink, to satisfy natural requirements and to procreate or, at least, to have sexual activity of one kind or the other. In that respect, there is little difference between a Mongol and a French man or between a Japanese young girl and an Italian one.

The differences arise when we look at the manner in which the needs are satisfied. The requirements of an Eskimo when it comes to food are not the same as those of a Spaniard simply because of the weather; but a greater consistency of behaviour is always there when we deal with sexual relations, regardless of diet.

The differences also arise when we try and analyse how those requirements are satisfied or those relations are given effect to in terms of locality, technique, and intensity of performance or of feeling.

The effect of the weather, especially the sun, on sexual relations should by no means be discounted. It is an undoubted fact that the English weather has marked consequences as far as the sexual behaviour is concerned of those who live in the British Isles. With warm fronts, cold fronts, occluded fronts, alternating at great speed over the whole country, it is not too easy for the body to keep up the various levels of energy and intensity that those fronts may have brought about. For example, rain and dampness are known to have a debilitating or at least disheartening, if not deflating, effect on many people.

We are becoming increasingly aware of the consequences that changes in pressure, humidity and temperature have on human beings. What were once considered old wives' tales are now being rehabilitated on a regular basis. The variations in temperature are particularly marked throughout the British Isles, consequently the individual energy levels are affected by a sort of tug-of-war. A sunny day or spell raises excitement, soon to be frustrated once the cloud cover reappears. It is true that not all individuals are affected in the same manner and to the same degree; but very often they are affected without even being aware of what is happening or indeed why.

Not to be discounted either is the consideration that less sunlight reduces the amount of vitamin D available to the body. It isn't clear whether any studies have been made to consider the effect of such reduction on sexual desire but it is here suggested that the effect exists and is much more significant that the English people (and northern people generally) are prepared to acknowledge. Only recently, in fact, have GPs been dedicating greater attention to the effects of vitamin D deficiencies.

Whilst most people are conscious of the fact that their bodily functions slow down in cold weather and are reactivated by the appearance of warmth (whether of the real kind resulting from a rise in temperature or of what one could term the psychological type brought about simply by the presence of a blue sky or a sunny day), most people would admit that they are more cheerful and more energetic when the sun is shining. This is obvious, of course.

It would be very odd indeed if the effects of variations in air pressure, humidity, temperature and light did not have a marked, almost magnetic, effect on the body's hormones and on its sexual organs; blood circulation is often at the mercy of weather changes. Whilst this applies to both men and women, it is here suggested that the effect is more noticeable, if not dramatic, where men are concerned: if the energy isn't there, the physical performance reduces, where it does not disappear entirely.

It is for these reasons that the thesis is here maintained that considerable weight must be attached to the unpredictable and possibly unique meteorological conditions prevailing in England. How could one explain otherwise the changes in mood and behaviour that come over Northern people as soon as they move, even for a short period, to warmer climes?

It is suggested that the inevitable and rather stoic habituation to England's weather conditions has had an exceptionally marked formative influence on our national character and has contributed to the creation of a typical kind of humour which is of great help nationally in the acceptance of difficult or unusual circumstances. It is a pity, however, as will be observed later, that such humour does not extend to sexual activity.

Definitely, we cannot discount the effect of the British weather on the sexual performance of the inhabitants of the British Isles. A further brief reference to the concept will be made in a later chapter.

It cannot be a coincidence, for example, that black men claim some kind of greater sexual prowess over their white counterparts. Whether they are right or wrong, it is difficult to disabuse them of that notion. It is hardly surprising that there is among certain strata of British society a fairly current and commonly used expression to the effect that once a woman has tried black, she will always go back!

That may or may not be true and no comment is passed here upon the validity, alleged or otherwise, of statements of this ilk; but the fact that they are made highlights a different approach to sexual relations, as well as the conceit of the black man in this field.

In the same manner, for instance, and quite unrelated to sexual relations, the French and the Italians claim superiority in matters of food; an Eskimo or a Tartar would not dare argue that their diet is better, or at least more interesting.

But leaving aside situations such as these, there is no doubt that when it comes to sexual behaviour generally there are some differences between people. We shall concentrate obviously on the behaviour of the English.

The description has already been applied to it as hypocritical. One should try and explain what is meant by the usage of such adjective, which is not necessarily offensive.

Before doing so, however, one should note the changes that are occurring in English girls. They are maturing at a much earlier date; it has been recorded that puberty in England is now not infrequent in girls as young as eight or ten years of age. This in itself creates problems, actual and psychological. Furthermore, girls themselves are more formed and usually taller than they were, say, even 20 years ago. In a different sense it could be said that they become young women at a much earlier date than their mothers or grandmothers and therefore are under greater pressure, both personally and socially, to indulge in intercourse sooner than one might expect and nature suggests.

There are other environmental and social reasons why this is happening.

As a result of such earlier maturity, they are encouraged increasingly to wear clothes which of themselves highlight their sexual attributes and nowadays may rely on the spread of sexual education and contraception.

A rather sad development is that children under the age of ten are being influenced by US-style mini-model parades with catwalks and what have become known as 'lipstick and limo' parties.

At the end of the day, however, it is here suggested that the primary cause of precocious sexual activity is lack of self-control.

The young girl of earlier times, who, coming through her pubescent phase, postponed the giving of herself, if such be the correct expression to use, until she felt ready for it, displayed a certain confidence in herself, which was evidence of a wish to project her development and maturity in one way or the other.

She clearly had taken a decision not to let outside factors influence her attitude; in other words, she must have felt that she had some kind of control over her sexuality and some concern, if not respect, for her own body. There are no figures that relate an early loss of virginity to bad dietary practices and, accordingly, obesity; but the possibility of a correlation between the two should not be discounted without further analysis in the same manner as one might wish to consider any connection between illnesses like bulimia and anorexia with an early start to sexual activity, let alone the situations of self-harm, binge drinking and the ever-increasing spread of Chlamydia resulting from an early start to sexual activity.

The absence of this kind of confidence and the resultant lack of self-control is also, in all likelihood, the cause of some of the extreme forms of behaviour displayed by our young English girls, such as the taking of drugs, the abuse of alcohol, manifestations of violence and, indeed, rage and irritation at other people, evidenced by the increasing examples of aggressive behaviour by women not merely under-age and whether at the wheel of a car or elsewhere.

Our society is reluctant to identify a causal connection between a very early loss of virginity and violent behaviour but it is not beyond the realms of possibility that there is a link there.

An increasingly common feature that appears to aggravate the relationship between the sexes is the availability of internet facilities. Added to the fairly extensive freedom available in the use of the printed word and television and film industries, these have resulted in an acceleration in the spread of pornographic material since we have moved from CD ROMS to DVDs, the latter allowing the viewer to become an active participant in the visual display by manipulating the posture and the viewpoint of the images on the screen. It can thus be stated unhesitatingly that pornography feeds on technology in the same way as technology feeds on pornography. In a strange sense, it could be said that as we have produced fast food, so we have offered the public fast sex, and we the English seem to thrive on both.

This development is commonly claimed to have a liberating influence on both men and women, in the sense that it allows them independent enjoyment. The interactivity of the viewer is regarded by some as a democratic development. It is often said that before an internet screen we are all equal whereas in the pursuit of sexual enjoyment, for one reason or another, some of us are more successful than others.

Furthermore, the modern view seems to be that women in particular ought to have sexual enjoyment without having to rely on any other person to whom they might become either too attached or enslaved. As the feminist Barbara Seaman has observed, 'woman is liberated by masturbation'[1]; by extension, the modern view is that man is similarly released from concern and responsibility for his female partner.

The vacuity of the assertion quoted is remarkable. What does it mean? Liberated from whom? Liberated from what?

If it is meant to convey the idea that woman is at long last liberated from her slavery to man then there is nothing new about the fact, such liberation having started in 1882 when the absolute control by the husband over his wife's property, and legal restrictions on her ownership of it, were at last abolished.

---

[1] *Barbara Seaman, 'Free & Female', Coward, McCann & Geoghegan Inc, New York, 1972*

If it means that she is at last liberated from the slavery of child-bearing, it is a pointless observation, given that, since the introduction of the Pill in 1961, as well as the use of other contraceptive means within the control of woman herself, she can no longer be forced to be a mother.

The principal criticism however is a different one. The statement highlights the predominance of clitoral satisfaction of sexual needs over the vaginal. If that be so, it ignores the mental, emotional and affective component which the psychological make-up and the physiology of woman introduce into any kind of sexual activity.

The assertion of the individual to be able to develop total control over his or her sexual activity by renouncing the participation of any other person is wholly unrealistic. It endorses the fact that more and more people are living alone: that is quite sad (as an aside, it is worth noting that according to statistics published recently – April 2011 – no less than 31% of habitable units in England are in the occupation of one person only. Later statistics – November 2012 – indicate that nearly 2.5 million adults between the ages of 45 and 64 live alone, such figure representing an increase of over 50% since 1996). Indeed, sadness, as has been observed, is a noticeable feature in the

English sexual scene and joyful behaviour before, during and after intercourse appears to be lacking. It could be said that modern English women are only too pleased to be shot of the man who in turn appears to be in a hurry to put his trousers back on (rather a different approach to intercourse by woman, one would suggest, from that prevailing in England in the 17th and 18th centuries).

The problem will be compounded because internet activity is global so that it doesn't matter where you live or what your culture or background are; you can very easily become enslaved in any part of the world.

These developments will ensure that pornography continues to spread and, in a strange sense, will endorse the increasing passivity of human beings who will all be turned into 'voyeurs'. In what one may term euphemistically 'the old days' if one was interested in pornography one had to become fairly active to obtain it, at least in England.

Steps had to be taken to look for it, to identify and either to take part in it or to purchase it. Thanks to the internet – and of course, thanks also to the increasingly sexual content and representation of all kinds of sexual activity proffered by most television channels – what we shall all have to do in less than a year or two (and what some of us are already doing) is to take steps actually to avoid pornography!

The combination of the electronic diffusion of books and what one can only term a form of literary voyeurism is creating a sort of collective sexual hysteria, which is evidenced, amongst other things, by the massive sales of any kind of sexually oriented publication, from magazines to pseudo-scientific books. The masses gloat over titillating, where not obscene, stories and descriptions of sexual activity, which are a perpetuation, in an ever-increasing manner, of an instinct that was always there. These manifestations of what is ultimately a form of a sexual impotence are accepted by our society without criticism; indeed, at times, also with a sneaking form of admiration for the creators of cheap descriptions especially of 'perverted' sexual activity which are totally unrelated to any form of feeling, if not love.

CHAPTER TWO – Sex in Society

Our Western society is highly sexualised. The sexualisation, however, is artificial in the sense that too many individuals and organisations have a vested interest, usually economic, in encouraging it. They increase demand for it and expectations of pleasure from it. Suffice it to think of the widespread availability of pornographic images, whether in films, newspapers, magazines, television, the internet. Even the encouragement of the use of contraceptive devices of one kind or the other, including, of course, the Pill, is often prompted more by monetary considerations than by concern for the well-being of young girls and society as a whole. It is interesting that it appears to be the practice, if not the law, that a young girl may ask for and may obtain the contraceptive pill whilst underage, often as early as aged 11 or 13, without the knowledge – let alone the consent – of her parents but if the same young girl (or youngster) is under the age of 18 and wants to have a tattoo (see the Tattooing of Minors Act 1969), she cannot lawfully since the tattooing of minors is expressly forbidden by that Act: surely some indication of a lack of balance, let alone common sense in our society.

The matter is aggravated by the fact that, for reasons of privacy, political correctness and whatever else is fashionable at the moment, the doctor who is approached for the Pill by a girl of say 13 will certainly not wish to communicate with her parents lest she or indeed others on her behalf might sue the prescribing doctor for breach of confidentiality.

It may not come amiss to observe in passing that not much attention has been dedicated by doctors and sociologists to the long-term effects of such an exceptionally early commencement of intercourse, as regards both the procreative ability and above all the libido of these young girls.

It may sound initially far-fetched but it is not to be ruled out that a very early start of intercourse may have long-term effects of which we are not at present aware.

The use of sexual aids has increased dramatically. Nowadays, they are more often called sexual toys, a euphemistic expression which is meant to favour acceptability and which will probably pave the way for their being sold in supermarkets.

This sexualisation is the national malaise. (Incidentally, it is also one of the major reasons which allowed Rupert Murdoch to have such power in an amoral and decadent society.)

It is not here suggested for one moment that some were not known even 3,000 years ago. There is plenty of evidence in the "sexual" verses of Greek writers and poets that dildos were well known, as witness the writings of such as Aristophanes and Herodas (or Herondas, as he is otherwise known).

The Romans knew even more about them than the Greeks, as witness the Roman writers Petronius and Propertius. Indeed, there seems to be precious little that we could teach the Romans in matters of sex since their degree of sophistication and understanding was very great indeed. Suffice it to mention the murals remaining at Pompei and the highly sexed, where not pornographic, verses of writers like Catullus, Juvenal, Lucretius, Martial and Ovid. They do not always make comfortable reading.

(The reader hardly needs reminding that nouns describing two fairly significant sexual activities, 'fellatio' and 'cunnilingus', are both Latin.)

Nowadays, however, the advent of technology has provided scope for much greater inventiveness and for solutions which could not possibly have been conceived even a hundred years ago.

Whilst the particular technological developments were probably inevitable they have had a very marked effect on the psychological reactions of the parties who use them.

As far as England is concerned, one must acknowledge that there are some extenuating factors. The Puritans are often blamed for the English attitude to sex, as are the Victorians, but such is the type of never-ending debate, which is not appropriate to a work of this format.

Nevertheless, there is ample foundation for the accusation by most Mediterranean and Arab people that the English attitude to sex is, in fact, highly hypocritical. One should at this stage explain what is meant here by hypocrisy: put rather simply, hypocrisy consists either in saying what one does not mean or in doing what one claims or pretends one does not or would not do.

There are many examples of the former type, which is quite common. Think of the husband who congratulates his wife who has just been to the hairdresser whereas deep down he thinks she looked a lot better before spending the money; or the pleasant remarks made to an invalid who is really looking unwell. That hypocrisy is quite harmless and in certain respects is at the root of good manners; clearly, it is not of the kind with which we are dealing when it comes to sexual relations.

The basic criticism, which many foreigners level at us when thinking of sexual relations, is that we are, or at least appear to be, ashamed of our bodies. There are, of course, examples to the contrary: the nudists, the exhibitionists and so on, but generally speaking the criticism is well founded.

We appear to fail to understand that sexual behaviour is an integral part of our personality and that to either be ashamed of it or to wish to hide it is in fact counter-productive. Typical of this approach is the long-standing argument that the private life of public figures should be their own and nobody else's. Obviously we all know that politicians, for example, say one thing and usually do another; equally, that there are men of the cloth whose private life does not live up to their sermons; or theorists who uphold the sanctity of marriage in their pronouncements who, in fact, have been divorced once or more often than that.

The argument that one should observe privacy about the sexual activities of public figures is, at least in the opinion of some (myself included, of course!), totally misplaced. The private life of public figures is as important as their public performance since the former inevitably influences the latter.

As an example, would we put a child molester in charge of a pack of Boy Scouts? Or install a convicted fraudster as managing director of a major bank?

It is much too easy to argue that private activity and public performance should be kept separate, at least in our society. Furthermore, it should not be forgotten that the insistence on the separation between private and public life is not due to any strong libertarian approach but rather to the fact that the majority of men in public life have skeletons in cupboards as far as their integrity and sexuality are concerned, which, if brought in to the public arena, would be damaging not only to them but also especially to their party and more particularly to any party which might be in power at the relevant time.

Take Prime Minister Herbert Asquith, who was Prime Minister during the First World War. Though married, he had a liaison with Venetia Stanley who was 35 years his junior. It was believed for a long time that such a relationship was purely platonic, but recently (April 2012) a biography of Asquith throws considerable doubt on such belief. It argues that it was an affair that was consummated and passionate and much upset Asquith's second wife Margot.

He was 63 and tried very hard to keep the relationship hidden and almost succeeded until Venetia Stanley got married, as the affair ended, and matters came to light.

Asquith appears to have written Venetia 560 letters at the time when, it is said, he should have been paying more attention to the war effort.

His successor, David Lloyd George, who followed him in 1916, had a long-standing relationship with Frances Stevenson who was a tutor to his daughter. That affair was anything but platonic and lasted over 40 years. It was well known and even though he was married, his escapade was tolerated and was hardly spoken of or reported by the Press. At the time, there were quite clearly different standards of morality and, hypocritically no doubt, though affairs of this nature obviously carried on as always, they were not really spoken of in public.

He married Frances Stevenson in 1943 after his wife had died.

It is worth observing at this point that the ability of the English to ignore adultery and other forms of sexual irregularity provided they remain secret, or at least private, is quite distinctive and can be said to have been a dominant social feature throughout the Regency, Victorian and Edwardian periods and, indeed, right up to the late 1950s/early 60s. It is best described as a typical manifestation of the sexual hypocrisy to which attention is being drawn.

Throughout the 17th, 18th and 19th centuries this lack of concern for private behaviour, no matter how improper, has alternated with phases of severity and criticism marked, when the sexual irregularities became public knowledge, by denigration and appeal to high moral principles, as well as punishment (often quite severe) for adulterers, fornicators and homosexuals (Oscar Wilde's treatment springs to mind).

We had to wait until the middle of the 20th century for more tolerant and 'liberal' views to manifest themselves. This liberalising phase started with the Wolfenden Report of 1954/57 (more about that later), which was followed by the 1967 legislation decriminalising private homosexual behaviour between consenting adults. The result of such legislation was the provision of a powerful voice to homosexuals in the same manner as the contraceptive pill has provided greater impulse to feminist and, indirectly, lesbian claims for equality of 'moral' consideration. Nowadays individual liberty and freedom of sexual behaviour have become the all important, if not the only, moral rule. Indeed, it can be said that the stage has now been reached when there is a reversal of attitudes. Christians (especially Catholics) can now complain with some justification that their 'human rights' are being sacrificed to male and female homosexual beliefs, practices, behaviour and claims to liberty of cult. That, however, is another story more suited to debate by politicians and sociologists than to detailed consideration in this small essay on English heterosexual trends.

It remains, nevertheless, a story that impacts on the sexual behaviour of the English and provides a discordant note when considering how we react to sex generally.

One need only consider, briefly, and merely as an example of the said hypocrisy (there are many others) the English, or should one say British, attitudes to prostitution and obscenity.

In this country, prostitution in itself, as we all know, is not illegal since women are allowed to sell their bodies. Running it as a trade, however, is.

A woman can turn her house into a place which may become a hive of sexual activity but, if she does it on her own, she cannot be prosecuted though her landlord may object. If two or more women band together, various laws can be made to apply to the same kind of behaviour and they may be criminally and civilly liable.

Of course, brothels are illegal. But anyone who knows places like London, Glasgow, Edinburgh, Liverpool, not to mention others, realises that they are effectively tolerated, if not encouraged. (Another example of our ability to tolerate private sexual irregularity provided it stays private and does not become public knowledge. Let us sweep it under the carpet and it will then disappear).

One of the most glaring examples of hypocrisy occurred when the committee chaired by Sir John Wolfenden CBE, nominated on August 27th 1954, reported three years later (September 1957). The committee was appointed 'to consider the law and practice relating to homosexual offences and to offences against the criminal law in connection with prostitution and solicitation for immoral purposes'.

The committee concluded that, contrary to previous practice, homosexual behaviour between consenting adults should no longer be a criminal offence. Perfectly proper.

As regards prostitution however, it endorsed what is termed in this work a hypocritical stance as far as matters sexual are concerned, because it recommended that whilst prostitution as such was not a crime, it should be made more difficult for the prostitutes to ply their trade openly in the streets.

Whereas under previous law one had to establish annoyance by the prostitute to her client (potential or actual) or to the general public, Wolfenden recommended that the law should be formulated so as to eliminate the requirement of annoyance, that maximum penalties for street offences should be increased and a system of progressively higher penalties for repeated offences should be introduced. Put differently, we should try to get the prostitutes off the streets by sweeping them under the carpet, disregarding completely the contrary recommendation of the Police, who would have preferred to know who the prostitutes were and where they could be found and feared that, as a result of that particular recommendation, they would disappear in places where, not being visible, they couldn't be identified so easily.

The point, however, that should be made is that whilst the committee took evidence from 35 professional and public bodies (the Churches, the British Medical Association, the Law Society etc), six government departments and 31 individual witnesses consisting of judges, magistrates, JPs, medical officers, etc, not a single prostitute was interviewed, no evidence whatever was taken from prostitutes. It is like asking a doctor to reach a conclusion as to an illness without examining the patient; the committee would certainly have learnt a lot about male sexual instincts by questioning one or more prostitutes. One must yield to the temptation of wondering whether its respectable members were perhaps afraid of what they might have been told. (I personally spoke to Lord Mischcon – then Victor Mischcon – in 1995 and he confirmed what is in any case a matter of record.)

The country's record on matters of obscenity is worse. The attacks on James Joyce's "Ulysses", the active persecution of DH Lawrence for his poems and, above all, for his "Lady Chatterley's Lover", are two reasonably modern and glaring examples of an inability to distinguish between freedom of expression and hypocritical repression. There may have been better justification for the prosecution of "Oz" and "Inside Linda Lovelace", to choose the two most obvious situations and one can perhaps understand the persecution of Marguerite Radclyffe Hall for "The Well of Loneliness" in the early part of the last century. The Sunday Times may have been right in claiming, way back in 1945, that Norman Mailer's "The Naked and the Dead" was offensive, as undoubtedly was Paul Ableman's "The Mouth and Oral Sex".

Until recently, lack of sexual education in schools was also blamed; again, that is arguable, and in any event there is now plenty of so-called sexual education in our schools, a point referred to later.

There is something in our genes that determines how we shall react to sex; education has only marginal effect. In turn, genes are governed by our psychological heritage and, particularly in the case of the English, by the uneven historical development of Christian beliefs, and affected by the weather.

The relevance of the weather has already been dealt with above and we are not alone in considering it. Many foreigners have suggested that the English attitude to sex is, in fact, a function of our weather. The British Isles are neither too hot nor too cold, governed by the Gulf Stream, shrouded as they were in fogs, at times, of the kind that allowed Jack the Ripper to move about freely or Sir Arthur Conan Doyle's characters to escape from

Holmes and Watson. This is an exaggeration, of course, but blue skies do give clarity to sexual activity, which is often lacking under dense clouds; dry heat provides a sexual drive which is unimpeded by social pseudo-restraints or rampant hypocritical attitudes, let alone any consideration of the impact on sexual performance of the softening effect of damp weather and overcast skies.

The essential problem with the English weather, one which does affect sexual performance, is its absolute unpredictability.

There is no longer (was there ever?) any clear distinction between the seasons (Byron had remarked that the English summer started in July to end in August...). We wake up one morning in glorious sunshine, full of the joys of life with anticipation for a successful day. Not too many hours later, the skies darken, the rain arrives and can stay for a long time.

It is here suggested that this unevenness creates havoc with one's sexual desires, excited by the sun and deflated by the rain. No serious study appears to have been made of the consequences of the weather on sexual performance, particularly of the male: perhaps it isn't worth the trouble.

This is apparent every time a northerner moves into a Mediterranean climate. It isn't the alcohol that makes him think that he will suddenly become God's gift to women, although that, of course, is a potent inducement: it is the sun, which dramatically offsets the softening effect of the damp English weather.

Our German cousins suffer from the same malady. For example, a pseudo medical book, which described eccentric sexual behaviour in great details, and was extremely popular in the second half of the 19th century in England, was written by the Viennese, Richard Krafft-Ebing, who was a psychiatrist. Havelock Ellis's editor, Villiers, was also German.

Iwan Bloch was the German historian of prostitution, one of the causes of which he attributed to physiological male masochism. He described at great length the obsession of the English with flagellation, which he considered a national trait going back to Anglo-Saxon origins, encouraged by the frequent beatings at English public schools; another cause is said to be the hardship of marine life, though that is more debatable.

Partly because of the influence of the weather, we have developed in England an attitude to matters sexual, which is hypocritically unrealistic, and is compounded by the fact that we seem to be quite unable to distinguish between different kinds of sexual relations. Furthermore, our constitutional fondness of the understatement often prevents us from applying the proper description to questionable conduct (the significance of such fondness will be considered in a later chapter).

Apart from these considerations, and well apart from the weather, of course (and leaving aside, for the moment, matters of religious belief), there are a number of other important factors that fall to be considered in identifying the probable causes of the unbalanced sexuality of the English people. Amongst these is the type of education which has been imparted to inhabitants of the British Isles in matters sexual over decades, and not only in schools. Put differently, the facts of life have been described and/or taught in a manner which has not only been unsatisfactory, but almost entirely twisted. The task of imparting sexual knowledge in the United Kingdom for quite some time has been entrusted to, or taken up by, visionaries who for one reason or another were themselves sexually unbalanced or impotent, or both. A few examples may serve to illustrate this concept.

CHAPTER THREE – Educational Sex

It is beyond my scope to consider in detail the disapproval of fellatio expressed by a number of religious beliefs and national customs. We should consider first the anonymous author in the 18th century of a book called 'Onania', a name he picked out of the bible (it is said in the book of Genesis – 38-6-10 – that Onan is punished by the Lord because of his misbehaviour. Nobody is certain what his misbehaviour was, it being often stated that it was because he didn't wish to give a child to his deceased brother's wife although a number of commentators think that it was masturbation). The invented term became synonymous with this particular activity, the author maintaining that masturbation weakened men.

The concept was picked up in either 1758 or 1770 by the Frenchman Tissot, whose book, in French, by the title "Onanisme" became a best-seller in Europe. Tissot as well maintained that masturbation, both for men and women, was to be avoided but he was particularly concerned about its weakening effect on men.

That was a premise for all that followed, English doctors even believing that masturbation led to illness and insanity and should be cured by simple foods and cold baths in the open air and, if they were insufficient, by prescribing sedatives like bromide. There is evidence that in the 19th century Isaac Baker Brown, a surgeon who operated in London, felt that women should be saved from this lonely and debilitating activity, and he carried out clitoridectomies (excisions of the clitoris) following the belief of the ancient that, in so doing, the sexual drive of woman would be reduced and her nymphomaniac tendencies could be cured, as well as her hysteria (and possibly even epilepsy). In this, he clearly showed his ignorance of women since there are some who are by nature nymphomaniacs and do not have recourse to doctors because of that...

(A barbarous, primeval practice, which was not made illegal in the UK until 2003 when the Female Genital Mutilation Act was passed.)

In the 18th century, we had a Scot, James Graham (born in 1745) who preached that impotence and sterility could be cured by sleeping in a 'celestial bed' of his invention, surrounded by odoriferous spices. One might of course think that this was merely a gimmick to make money; not so. He really believed it. He also campaigned to suppress prostitution, preached that sexual success and virility could only be obtained through a strict dietary discipline, reaching the conclusion, which most meat eaters would gladly challenge, that only vegetarians are sexy! A fad for vegetarianism, you may think. Not quite, for he said that in order to add to one's sexual prowess, human beings should bathe their genitalia every night and morning in cold water… brr, brr…!

He thought that prostitutes were the enemy of society, but the greatest evil was masturbation, and anyone who wanted to increase sexual powers, was required to abstain from sexual intercourse for varying periods of time, but essentially as long as one could. Try telling that to present day youngsters!

A separate though related concern was shared by Walter Matthew Gallichan who, in 1918, published "A Textbook of Sex Education". According to Gallichan, the "unfit" should be sterilised, masturbation had to be avoided at all costs because a waste of the seminal fluid provoked man into developing both a dull mind and a languid body. He obviously must have disagreed with the French writer Montaigne who remarked that 'vessels have to be emptied'…

To facilitate the lack of excitement, one should control one's diet avoiding foods that might have an aphrodisiac effect, and tight clothing, which might stimulate the body. He went so far as to argue that the wearing of corsets caused heightened and, as he put it, degenerate sexual feelings. A fetishist himself? All theoretical in any event, for in his view most women suffered from sexual apathy and coldness as a result of "feminine congenital sexual frigidity"!

There were other interesting characters in this field. One William Acton (1813-1878), a urologist, propounded the view that women were not interested in sex and that they only submitted to intercourse in order to have children (in his own words, "the majority of women are not much troubled by sexual feeling of any kind." Would you believe it?). He too argued that masturbation was an evil thing, especially for children and his teaching caused what became known at the time as "masturbation hysteria", evidence of which can be found in the gadgets that were manufactured to be applied to the genital area, some of which can be still be seen in museums.

He certainly showed that he didn't have a clue what he was talking about when he maintained that many females never feel any sexual excitement whatsoever, know little about sexual indulgence and if, and insofar as they have intercourse with their husbands, they do it either to please him or to have children. If it weren't for those two aims, they wouldn't be interested in any sexual activity whatsoever. Pardon?

Nor can one possibly agree with him when he argued that nymphomania was a form of insanity and that nymphomaniacs should be locked up in a lunatic asylum. His views echoed the Victorians' attitude to prostitution. The Metropolitan Police Act 1839 equated the common prostitute with the street walker and, of course, they were both to be punished. The Contagious Diseases Act 1846 and the Police Clauses Act 1847 began by highlighting the association between prostitutes and venereal disease, thus anticipating features of the approach to prostitution in most European countries, which persist to this day and were only reformed in England thanks to the efforts of Josephine Butler. These laws were not wholly repealed until 1886.

As far as he was concerned, both men and women, but obviously men in particular because wives were not "very much troubled with sexual feelings of any kind", should "sober down", effectively becoming more like their wives who, being modest women, did not desire any sexual gratification for themselves and insofar as they submitted to sexual intercourse, did so only to please their husbands and if it weren't because they wanted children, would abstain altogether... Try telling that to a modern young woman!

He thought that masturbation led to most diseases, including consumption and insanity, weakened muscles and acne (in the case of acne, in all likelihood having no scientific evidence whatsoever as to the process of causation).

Working along the same lines, John Laws Milton directed that a light wire cage should be placed over the genital areas to ensure that these particular types of evil were avoided. The degree of sophistication reached by him in the kind of equipment that he suggested would keep men and women sexually healthy, is so great that one should spare the reader's blushes by glossing over it.

Another propounder of unusual theories to govern our sexual activities was Richard Carlile (1790-1843) cited by Prof. Thomas Laqueur in his book "Making Sex – Body and Gender from The Greeks to Freud" (Harvard University Press 1992, p.229) who was strongly critical of masturbation, both male and female, and of prostitution.

He felt that 'the solitary vice' and the passions that led them towards prostitution could be controlled by the creation of 'Temples of Venus', which would assuage the extramarital satisfaction of both men and women whilst at the same time reducing, if not eliminating, masturbation that led to diseases of body and mind.

Like others in this field, his forecast proved wrong because modern woman is quite freely available but prostitution still flourishes.

On the other hand, Isaac Baker-Brown concentrated on self-abuse by the female sex. He claimed that it didn't exist, a fairly novel notion, and certainly one that will bring laughter to the rubicund face of most healthy philanderers and all exasperated feminists, especially those in the Anglo-American world.

At this stage one might be excused for believing that such absurd notions, though perhaps forgivable in centuries past, could no longer prevail in the 20th century. But, here in England, it gets worse as we move with the times.

Those who have sought and endeavoured to impart knowledge were not always motivated by altruism. Havelock Ellis, for example, the most important reporter of fairly aberrant sexual behaviour, after very many difficulties, succeeded in having his "Studies on the Psychology of Sex" published in London by Heinemann in 1906. In the six volumes that record his professional experience, he collates most of the notions that existed before him and is, on many issues, quite modern in outlook. The difficulty is, however, that he was in turn obsessed by his own sexuality, which was the result of a particular need for excitement to make up for his own deficiencies.

The problem about the credibility of Havelock Ellis's work is that he was impotent, even though he endeavoured to find reassurance. The whole of Chapter 2 in volume I is headed "The Art of Love". It runs from page 507 to page 575 and considers the physical aspects of lovemaking by identifying the different number of methods of intercourse selected by writers before him (such as Aretino and Forberg). Pages 376 to 476 from the same volume are dedicated to what he calls "undinism". A further 30 pages or thereabouts are included on the same subject and this time he uses a different word, "urolagnia", in the chapter headed "Mechanism of Sexual Deviation". The reader will be hard put to find the two nouns "undinism" and "urolagnia" in the dictionary since they were coined by Havelock Ellis and are not officially recognized in the English language.

They are meant to represent the causes and benefits of sexual enjoyment in watching women urinating. (Nor is this a neglected idea: in the 1990s we have seen at least one well-known Hollywood film portrayal of a popular actress urinating.)

Reassurance of his masculinity he found not only in writing his book but also by displaying his sperm to Olive Shreiber under the microscope, pointing out the motility of the cells[2]. One is bound to wonder, however, whether Havelock Ellis was really qualified at all to teach anybody anything about sex. Nevertheless, one should be grateful to him for reminding us of the comparison that Balzac made when he equated the husband making love to his wife to an orang-utan trying to play the violin!

Credit where credit is due, of course, but Havelock Ellis is the first of the 'notable urophiliacs' in the Wikipedia section (heading urolagnia) where he is described as having been 'impotent until the age of 60 when he discovered that he was aroused by the sight of a woman urinating', which bears out the classification given to him in this work.

We know that for most of his life the only form of lovemaking he indulged in was of the non-penetrative kind. He did get married

---

[2] *The New Women and the Old Men by Ruth Brandon, Secker & Warburg, London, 1989, page 37*

to Edith but, perhaps understandably, it would now appear that she had lesbian tendencies.

One must challenge strenuously his qualifications to teach anybody about sex, also because his judgement has proved suspect in many respects. The most obvious one is evidenced by the forecast he made sometime in 1910 that, given that women would eventually come to control their own sexual lives (he was right on that, of course), prostitution would decline, become unnecessary and, indeed, also inappropriate. One wonders what he would do a century later if he were visiting some areas of London or other major cities in the United Kingdom, or elsewhere throughout the world (eg. Amsterdam, the parks of Paris, the Ramblas in Barcelona, the banks of the Tiber in Rome etc).

Then we had Mrs Pankhurst's daughter, Christabel (1885-1958), a pillar of the women's liberation movement and an advocate of social reform, arguing that the complex seminal fluid should be conserved and not squandered by sexual activity because it had an invigorating influence; such conservation would enable men to develop noble feelings. It is not known whether she had read St Augustine, who referred to the divinity of semen ("semen hominis quiddam divini"). Clearly he meant that, in the process or act of reproduction, man partook of the divine.

As God created man, man himself, with the concurrence of woman, was allowed to create life in a godlike fashion. Such a profound and maybe even poetic description sounds rather quaint to modern ears; the contraceptive pill has taken away whatever divinity might have been attached to intercourse, almost like a chemical castration of modern man and recent technology has further downgraded semen by allowing its encapsulation and storage for use at any time. But who reads St Augustine's works nowadays?

Christabel Pankhurst certainly didn't like the men who resorted to prostitutes for practices that their wives wouldn't tolerate and for what she termed "unnatural abuses" of the sex function. She obviously could not have read Freud, who is on the record as saying that the only unnatural sexual activity is no sex at all.

She was not the only woman concerned with matters sexual. Mary Wollstonecraft, one of the principal feminists, well known not only for her errant private life but above all for her books, wrote in "Vindication of the Rights of Women" that '...women had the capacity to lead almost bodiless existences' (she is of course referring to sexual activity here) and despite the bad habits that they acquire at boarding school she did not believe in the existence of any strong sexual desire in women; an advantage no doubt, for woman could then concentrate more keenly and successfully on social remedies and on politics. She truly believed that, because of this, women had a mission to civilise men.

She expressed her views in her writings, especially her two principal works, "The Vindication of the Rights of Men" (1790) and "The Vindication of the Rights of Women" (1792); in the former she attacked men, and in the latter she eulogised women. She is hailed as the first feminist but she is not really a good example to be quoted so often since some of her views are quite suspect. Two examples will suffice: she was offended by the concept that some women were prostitutes (this is one element in the man/woman equation which really hurts for those feminists who, like her, assert the superiority of women over men). She argued that there was no real difference between a prostitute and a wife because they both had to work for a man; and that the only possible difference between them was the way in which women were, in fact, treated by men (or as a more modern feminist has put it – Dale Spender, "Women Have Ideas", Pandora, 1982, page 480 – "women's work '...was to trade their bodies on a casual basis (prostitute), a semi-permanent basis (mistress) or a permanent basis (wife)'..."). Mary Wollstonecraft is also on the record as saying in "A Vindication of the Rights of Women" – 'I do not wish women to have power over men; but over themselves'. A statement which sounds good enough at first blush but is based on the misconception that people who acquire power will not use it. Those who claim power over themselves normally end up by exercising their power over others and in the case of women, if they acquire power they will use it over men, since power is not something that one puts in the safe and looks at once a year.

Leaving aside the theoretical aspects of her argument, however, it is a matter of record that she led such a scandalous life that one is entitled to say – as in the other instances quoted in this chapter and elsewhere in this book – that the sermons come from the wrong pulpit.

She left England very young after a disappointing love affair and went to Paris where she met an American, Gilbert Imlay, with whom again she embarked upon an amorous relationship. It was equally unsuccessful. She then returned to London where she met an artist, Henry Fuseli, to whom she initially suggested a threesome. With him she had an illegitimate child.

Her life was clearly unhappy. She tried to commit suicide twice, once by taking an overdose of laudanum and the second time by jumping into the River Thames. She was rescued.

She then married William Godwin of whom it can be said that he rendered her quite a disservice when, after her death, he published a most unflattering biography of the 'First Feminist'. She is always referred to as Mary Wollstonecraft save on her tomb where her name is shown as Mary Wollstonecraft-Godwin.

The tendency to turn women into creatures lacking sexual passion was picked up by Sarah Ellis who in her work "The Wives of England" argued that women are less affected by sexual passion than men and as a result had greater tranquillity of body and therefore of mind.

In fact, she was most insistent in her urging women to be strong like men. As a result, they should at all costs control their emotions. She did not seem to appreciate that one of the consequences of the constant efforts to control emotions would be a psychological repression that was to remain with English women for a very long time.

Another questionable view was that of Keith Vaughan who, before the Second World War, became known for his homosexual/masochistic tendencies and for all sorts of forms of self-inflicted genital torture, such as, for example, electric shocks.

Even such a high-principled medical practitioner as Mary Scharlieb (born 1845), a devout Anglo-Catholic who started out in private practice in 1887 against many odds and much prejudice, could not resist the temptation of arguing that contraception led to madness.

This is not a criticism of a fundamentally honest and religious woman who consistently opposed divorce (the Matrimonial Causes of 1857 had not long been passed despite opposition. It introduced the concept of fault, leading to divorce, that would last for well over a century; that it is to say until it was superseded by the Divorce Reform Act of 1969, which effectively made divorce available on demand).

James Scott, who wrote in 1899, maintained that women did not want nor knew how to enjoy sex. He listed what he thought were the sins against nature (masturbation, coitus interruptus, oral/genital sex, homosexuality and bestiality) he too maintaining that masturbation weakened men.

One of the groups that had great impact on our sexual customs, and on British society in the 20th century, became known as "The Bloomsbury Set". The description is almost pleasant, for it conjures up pictures of a fairly respectable and easy-going group of people in a civilised London district, associated with the British Museum, so that the reader who knows nothing about the characters who composed the particular group might think that they were generous artists, pleasant painters, and sensible intellectuals, probably with Cambridge degrees, who had a positive contribution to make to the well-being of Great Britain. Indeed, some of the names of those involved are quite familiar and sound very good: E M Forster, John Maynard-Keynes, Roger Fry, Clive Bell, Duncan Grant, Arthur Hobhouse, Lytton Strachey, George Bernard Shaw, Sidney Webb, Leonard Wolf, and George Moore. And some of the women (but is that the right description of them?) – Virginia Woolf, Vanessa Bell, Beatrice Webb, Violet Trefusis, Rosamund Grosvenor, Mary Campbell, Dora Carrington.

It is difficult to share such a view. Some might argue that they were a fairly rotten bunch, Shaw perhaps excepted. It is beyond the scope of this work to consider the individuals in detail. But picking out at random what they said and/or did, one should not forget that Lytton Strachey objected violently to Britain's stance during the 1914-18 War. He was a conscientious objector who thought that the war was brought about by the influence of our Victorian values, which would in due course lead civilisation to slaughter and, worse still, went on record as saying that he didn't much care about England being victorious.

E M Forster, who wrote "A Passage to India", had always made it quite clear that he would sooner betray his country than his friends, and was a well-known homosexual, as indeed was Strachey. English society cannot be too proud of Forster. His lack of patriotism was fairly well known and he failed completely to understand that the Victorian values which he and his fellow members of The Bloomsbury Set so openly and violently criticised, were those that had served the country in good stead and had enabled it to create an empire. The values that they advocated and the conduct in which they indulged, namely homosexuality, lesbianism, and the most utter disregard of the family, let alone of outmoded concepts like patriotism, loyalty, honesty, duty, and so on, were of the kind that have got Britain where it is at the beginning of the third millennium, namely a country which no longer has an Empire, has lost its sense of history, that doesn't understand in what direction it should move, obsessed by sex and violence and destructive of the only social unit that might in fact still save it, namely the family. But that is a different story.

If all these people had lived privately and quietly in Bloomsbury it wouldn't have mattered very much. But they made their views and their behaviour well known publicly and had a very negative effect on the country. Indeed, it has been claimed[3] – it is somewhat awkward to decide how convincingly – that their attitudes to Germany and to Russia may have seriously contributed to the Second World War.

One should not be too concerned about the political consequences of their behaviour, but the respect which is still paid to them nowadays either in spite, or more probably because, of their behaviour, is a mark of our utter English inability to understand that the sexual behaviour of individuals not only influences their public performance, their judgment and their usefulness to the country, if they are public figures, but also creates an aura of acceptability and respectability which is reflected in the compulsive and promiscuous nature of present-day sexual tendencies and behaviour, both for men and for women (incidentally, this misunderstanding is a principal reason

---

[3] *Andrew Roberts in "The Eminent Churchillians", Phoenix 1995*

why we are so keen to endeavour to separate and keep secret their private from their public life as evidenced by the constant abuse in recent years of the so-called 'gagging' injunctions; the point has already been made above but in the opinion of this writer at least, requires belabouring).

Put differently, anybody who follows the tenets of The Bloomsbury Set has a perverted view of sexuality, and above all, of life. The concepts that they propounded of the greatest freedom for the individual in matters sexual and the irrelevance of any kind of morality, have resulted in the hedonistic view of behaviour which is a marked feature of our society.

A dose of some of the Victorian values which we conspicuously lack, would nowadays serve England in very good stead. When politicians speak about our economic evils, they fail completely to see that they mostly stem from the disregard of morality and of honour, which, in turn, is the result of a wholly ill-considered and ignorant approach to matters sexual; but one shouldn't sermonise.

CHAPTER FOUR – Sermons from the Wrong Pulpit

Our "greatest" reformer of the 20th century in matters sexual is Marie Carmichael Stopes, towards whom many people may well have cause to feel grateful because of her support for contraception; but she was even less qualified to preach to them than any of the persons previously referred to.

She is worthy of closer attention (and that is why she has been left almost until last) if for no other reason that the myth appears to be perpetuated in the UK that the work she did was of great comfort for humanity. That view is not shared here: the propounder of the rights of women and the teacher of sexual practices for youngsters, was an unbalanced person with marked male characteristics, or so Keith Briant, one of her biographers, maintains[4]. Most persons would assume that she was a doctor of medicine; or possibly a sociologist or a psychotherapist. Not at all: she was a science graduate whose initial specialisation was the study of coal... She had a rather complex personality. For example, she thought she was beautiful and sexy but was absolutely deluded about her appearance. Films and photos of the period show that she was rather imperfectly formed, was overweight, rather masculine looking, and physically unattractive. She had her first love affair at 19 with a Japanese

---

[4] *A Biography" – the Hogarth Press 1962*

professor. One uses the term "love affair" because it is an expression which is so popular in the English language; but in context, it is quite meaningless. It continued until she was 28 and, as far as anybody knows, it resulted in nothing more positive than meetings, not that often, and exchanges of correspondence.

At 31 she married and at 32 she was divorced: the marriage was annulled because of non-consummation. Sexually frustrated, she searched for the limelight and in 1918 (she was still a virgin at the time) she published "Married Love"; her book was an immediate success. It ran to 26 editions and sold more than one million copies worldwide. It is no coincidence that it was published one month after the women of the UK were given the vote. A virgin with one failed marriage thus became, for England, an authority on sex: could we term her the first agony aunt?

At 34, she had a child who died at birth. Her only son was born to her when she was 43. Her relationship with him was very odd. She did not approve of his marriage because his wife had a small eye-sight problem and didn't even attend it; indeed, she refused to see him even when, in 1958, she was dying at the age of 78 (incidentally, she thought she would live to be 120 because she was communing with God, He having decided that she was to be his prophet). It is fascinating to consider how people can believe that they have the privilege of speaking to the Almighty; the odd one crops up from time to time; most of them are unbalanced.

On 15th March 1921, she established her first birth control clinic offering the cervical cap. Although she believed that the 'elite' women of England were not producing enough children, she objected to too many children being born to the lower classes. She advocated selective breeding by sterilisation on what one may call Nazi principles. She maintained that the only children who were to be bred and who, in turn, had any right to breed, would have to be healthy, beautiful and intelligent; the rest, as at Sparta, could be destroyed at birth, even assuming that, despite her clinics, they ever got that far. There is no doubt about her approach to the so-called purity of the race. Even a cursory glance at page 30 of one of her books, *Wise Parenthood*[5], shows the concept quite clearly. She obviously had never heard of crossbreeding, of the need to import new blood; equally, she can't have known that, for example, Leonardo da Vinci was illegitimate, as were many others, who deserve a far greater place in history than is apparently provided to her.

---

[5] *Putnam & Co. 1918*

She is often hailed as a great feminist but her mission was not so much to help poor women, as to produce a great new era of human evolution. Pure Utopia.

As far as one can assess from Briant's biography, she was retarded in her development by her father's concern for her and her first relations with anyone at all, which started at 19, were in the main with older women. It is not suggested that they were of a sexual nature because apparently they were not; but that doesn't make the position any better. A principal relationship was with M.S. whom she called "Psyche, my beloved". Her sexual frustration, as far as can be made out, was quite great, bearing in mind that it would appear – one can put it no higher because, after all, who knows? – that her loss of virginity occurred rather late in life, at the age of about 30.

Hardly had she got married, than a more or less "ménage à trois" was established with Aylmer Maude. Her sexual relations with her husband were totally unsatisfactory. At the age of 58, when she had not had the opportunity – one dares not call it pleasure – of having sex with him for 5 years, he wrote her a note indicating that he would allow her to have affairs. Whether this offer was taken up or not, her biographer Briant does not say. Modern research propounds to the view that the particular letter that set up the triangular affair was written at her instigation and under dictation by her, she being desirous of feeling "free".

Some of her ideas were absolutely mad. In 1924, aged 44, she argued (how could she know?!) that the normal style of trousers was bad for her son's genital organs so special culottes were made for him... In the same year she wrote the book by the title "Enduring Passion", at a time when her own marriage was already crumbling.

This book was supposed to teach people how to preserve a marriage and keep up the sexual interest in it. It is hardly surprising that very many of the agony aunts of modern times do exactly the same when their personal relations and, above all, their marriages, if they haven't already collapsed, are on the verge of doing so. For example, at page 86 in Married Love[6] she says "The modern, civilised, neurotic woman has become a byword in the Western world. Why? I am certain that much of suffering is caused by the ignorance of both men and women regarding not only the inner psychology but even the obvious outward expression of the complete sex act". This may have been true in 1918, but nearly a century later there is no

[6] *The Hogarth Press 1918*

ignorance, in the UK at least, about the nature of the sex act; but one is entitled to ask how successful are our sexual relations in the year 2013?

But look at another one: on page 93 of the same work, she recommends, with a view to maintaining the sense of novelty and excitement in a marriage and to eliminating the triviality that follows upon the intimacy of the parties sharing a bedroom or a bathroom or whatever, that "whenever the finances allow, the husband and wife should have separate bedrooms; failing that, they should make use of a curtain which can and will be drawn so as to divide the room they share". No comment.

It is possible that Marie Stopes did not initially realise the consequences of what she was doing. In theory, her aims were not unsound. She preached the emancipation of women from the slavery of having unwanted children in order that the woman might enjoy her marriage and her children: a thoroughly commendable principle. She certainly did not approve of permissiveness and was very careful about the people she mixed with, even though she did not object to homosexuals, as her campaigns on behalf of Lord Douglas show. But she failed completely to understand the import of what she preached. She did not herself approve of promiscuity of any kind but did not, initially at least, draw the logical conclusion from her teaching, namely that contraception may actually encourage promiscuity, any more than she realised that by making woman "mistress of her own body" – what a horrid expression that is – she would cause certain men to be terrified of women and thus make them express more openly their latent homosexuality.

She set out to make people happier in their marriages – a thoroughly commendable aim – but failed to realise that contraception would give some women the kind of freedom that makes them restless and therefore less likely to be happy as married partners, as witness, amongst other things, our ever-increasing rate of divorce.

She did not like men to use contraceptives, the reason being her belief, first expressed in the book "Married Love" and repeated later on, that the secretions accompanying men's semen were highly beneficial when absorbed by women. She was laughed at initially, but others started to go along the same road. One must admire her dislike of any kind of sexual immorality and acknowledge that, despite the disbelief voiced at the time by many, as regards this particular benefit of heterosexual intercourse, she was quite right. The belief is certainly shared in most countries and has been vindicated by modern science. It is now accepted that man's semen contains comparatively high traces of zinc, a mineral which is much needed, especially by women. The obvious, by modern standards, chemical benefit to woman also explains, as least in part, the accepted sadness which touches man after intercourse. Psychologists and scientist had initially believed that such sadness, identified very many years ago by the Romans, ("Post Coitum Omnis Homo Tristis" which freely translated means that after ejaculation, man feels a sense of loss, which results in a minor form of sadness) was due to the fact that man had parted with something that was intimately associated with him and, as some had suggested, felt that he had been tricked by woman into doing so. Present scientific discoveries put it in a better perspective: the "sadness" is both physical (chemical) and psychological.

Her insistence that morality was not the outcome of fear, but an intrinsic part of human nature, was almost the belief of a Catholic. She set out to determine that only beautiful, healthy, intelligent children should be born, failing completely to realise that the last person who would propound the same principle, namely Hitler, himself an unbalanced sexual personality (was this because he only had one ball...?!), would, to put it mildly, have achieved a world of zombies if he had had his way. In fact, one of the main criticisms of Marie Stopes is that in her bully-like attitude she failed to manifest any kind of vision.

All in all, she preached an apparently brilliant sermon in a field where she herself was a hopeless failure. Because such sermons were the result of her frustration, they had the determination and the conviction of the fanatic, but they lacked the perception and intelligence of the balanced. It was for the first time in 1956, two years before her death, (see her preface to the 29th edition of "Married Love") that she began to voice her disillusionment ("Alas, today, over-emphasis on sex has become one of the features of the less serious newspaper press….; nowadays the normal does not supply the necessary "spiciness" for flare-head articles in the popular press. And we suffer today a popularising of over-emphasised sex verging on, if not actually, abnormal and unpleasant"). She got there a little bit late.

CHAPTER FIVE – More Sermons from the Wrong Pulpit

Some of the ideas of Marie Stopes, especially that of separate beds, at least at the commencement of any marriage, were echoed in 1924 by another female writer, Isabelle Hutton. In her book "The Hygiene of Marriage" she focussed on the fact that, in the early part of the 20th century, most brides were virgins and many of them quite ignorant of the implications of married life in sexual terms. As a result, quite a number of marriages were not consummated because the parties did not really understand what sex was all about. The situation in fact remained roughly the same until just before the Second World War. Accordingly, Isabelle Hutton maintained that separate beds were a necessity because innocent brides were quite unprepared to face the strength of the erect penis and that it took them a very long time indeed to become sexually excited even if there had been penetration on their first night (an observation that does in fact apply to some women).

Undue attention has, perhaps, been dedicated to Mary Stopes but she was, and is, so well known and her birth control clinics played such a major part in the development of the sexual 'mores' of England in particular that she could not too easily be ignored.

Of course, it isn't for a moment suggested that what she wrote has any significance in the third millennium; but she provoked a number of ripples on the sea of tranquillity of England's sexuality, which were to result in much greater waves being produced at a later date.

It is worth recording at this stage that the situation may not have been quite as the majority of these 'creatures' described. They were in the main of middle class extraction and their observations related to the people of the towns and cities. The position in the countryside had, for centuries, been quite different and virginity was much more easily lost there than in the cities.

The novelist Peter Vansittart records that round about the 18th century there was a popular jingle in the countryside, which went:

> *"Here lies the body of Mary Charlotte,*
> *Born a Virgin, died a Harlot;*
> *Until fifteen she kept her Virginity,*
> *Which is a record in this Vicinity."*

Another personality that cannot be ignored when it comes to matters sexual is Eustace Chesser. In 1941 he wrote his book "Love Without Fear", a guide to sexual techniques. There was nothing new about what he propounded, but the mere fact that he wrote it in non-medical jargon was enough to get him prosecuted for pornography, though he was acquitted.

He gave evidence to the Wolfenden Committee, which (see above) reported on homosexuality and prostitution. He was a psychiatrist, but also an abortionist and one of the few who, in his day, felt able to state openly, when he was called in 1972 to give evidence for the defence in the Lady Chatterley's Lover obscenity trial, that pornography is good for you. But even so his views are quite suspect. In another book he wrote, "Is Marriage Necessary?"[7], he says in terms (p.87) "contraception and legalised abortion will in time reduce the number of unwanted children to negligible proportions. They are unlikely to be so numerous that adoption presents a difficulty". Anyone reading him at the time would have accepted this statement as reasonable and logical. Given the fantastic increase in illegitimate births in the United Kingdom since 1974 (a situation considered in greater detail later), one is entitled to cast considerable doubt on the validity of his thinking. Perhaps he can

---

[7] *reprinted by W H Allen London 1974*

be excused on the ground that he wasn't really English. His parents were Jewish and had come to Scotland from Russia; but he enjoyed great notoriety in his day, even though not everybody accepted his view as to the therapeutic value of pornography and of masturbatory activity.

His notoriety continued with the sexual emancipation of women during and after World War II and the advent in the UK of the contraceptive pill in 1961.

October 2012 saw the reissue in somewhat revised form of a book that proved very popular in the English-speaking world, "The Joy of Sex" written 40 years previously by Dr Alex Comfort.

He died in March 2000 after a very busy life of study and argument and had a number of medical qualifications. The purpose of the work was clearly educational but even he, in true English style, allowed himself to be carried away when describing as joyful certain types of sexual activity which, to put it mildly, are clearly inconvenient. For example, he said that sexual relations could be had both on a motorbike (stationary or moving) and on horseback (cantering or galloping). The former is clearly a potentially dangerous exercise apart from the complications it may give rise to depending upon who rides pillion; the latter, again depending on who rides in front, presupposes a physical prowess, at least on the part of man, which is probably somewhat difficult to come by.

For years, we have seen the growth in this country of writers and agony aunts with skeletons in cupboards, doctors who falsely claim to have found the secret of marital success, and actresses and journalists who are perfectly content to go into print and tell everybody else how they should run their lives, sexual or otherwise, despite being utter failures in their own personal relations. However, the advice and the sermon come from the wrong pulpit. We have in England – and by extension in the Western world – a whole mystique about sexual relations which stems from the teaching of persons who know nothing whatsoever about sex and yet profess to be able of giving advice. If I want to know how to make money, I seek the assistance of a Rothschild or, indeed, of anybody else who has proved how to make money because he/she has made it; I do not listen to what a “bum” or “down-and-out” tells me in the pub. If I want to know what is wrong with my cow, I listen to an experienced stockman or to a vet but I do not go and consult any budding Oscar Wilde; if I need advice on the law, I go to an experienced solicitor but I certainly don’t listen to what a fiddler in a jazz band tells me; if I am ill, I consult a doctor or a specialist but I don’t go to a quack or listen to old wives tales; if I want a heart transplant, I go to a reputable surgeon and not to the local butcher. In other words, it seems sensible that one should go to those who earn a living successfully out of what they do for advice on the specific subjects in which they specialise; alternatively, one should go to those who have made a success of their affairs or their relations.

If we need guidance to a successful marriage, we certainly should not go and consult Joan Collins or Zsa Zsa Gabor. By parity of reasoning, if we want to know how to bring up our children, we do not seek the opinion of a person who has never had any. After all, would it be wise to put a vegetarian in charge of the Meat Marketing Board?

The problem about most of those who seem to relish giving sexual and marital advice is that few of them are qualified to tell others what to do. A few examples of their incompetence in the sexual sphere will suffice; and yet, they are popular guides to sex, marriage and happiness.

A well-known agony aunt, writing in a daily newspaper with high circulation, claimed to have answered tens of thousands of letters from agonising women, mostly, and possibly some men, and purported to give them advice on their sexual life, marital problems, etc. It is well known that her husband had been having an affair for very many years indeed without her knowledge.

Not too long ago another well-known woman, much in the public eye, wrote a book by the title "The Fun Don't Stop". It is a sort of self-help book which most young ladies may well be tempted to read, but the wisdom that she endeavoured to impart does sound a little odd for a mother of three who was having an affair with a popular singer. What her "saintly" husband may have thought about her, we are in no position to determine. But the advice sounds rather hollow and who knows how many times she may have woken up in the middle of the night haunted by the very words she wrote in her book. Given that her husband was a saint she may have preferred a "sinner" like the person she committed adultery with. That highlights the dichotomy between love and lust but hardly provides the credentials for trying to teach others how to live.

At her third attempt to make a success of marital life, a well-known actress wrote her "Guide to Romantic Living". Again, one must wonder how many romantically inclined young ladies have rushed to purchase such an important contribution to knowledge given that we all know that her spouse was anything but a perfect husband. He appears to have had a drink and drugs problem and may well have appreciated less fragrant women than his wife.

It is easy to forgive these writers because they had no technical and professional medical qualifications. The same cannot be said of a well-known doctor, now on her third marriage, for no sooner had she published her book "The Magic of Sex" – and the title says it all – than her husband joined up with a well-known actress.

Given that the subject matter of her book encompasses the mechanics of sex and suggestions of what steps women should take to keep their men (soft hands, clean and shiny hair, etc.) one can't help feeling that there seems to be a curse upon those persons who bare their souls in public, with a view either to showing off how good and successful they are, or educating others, or for profit.

The marriage of a TV presenter did not fare much better, when she discovered after sixteen years that her surgeon husband was having an affair.

Another TV actress has had a rather chequered career, her first marriage ending after seven years, her second after eleven, and her private life being somewhat questionable, and not of the kind that a sensitive young girl would wish to imitate; or perhaps, exactly the reverse, because on the same day as the Daily Mail (11 October 2001) published a fairly comprehensive review of the private lives of agony aunts, it also contained a section in its "Femail" magazine highlighting how alcohol abuse amongst middle class young women is now an epidemic in England, and quoting one as saying that she needed "four vodkas and four gins on a Saturday just to help make me feel normal".

The last example is even better known, namely the author of a book published in 1969 by the title "How to Stay Married". A highly commendable theme, although, perhaps entirely by coincidence that year saw the passing of the Divorce Reform Act, which made divorce on demand available in the United Kingdom (and in fact is the tombstone marking the burial of the English family and, with it, English society), and the appointment by Barbara Castle of the Finer Commission[8], which without any parliamentary authority whatsoever, established the classification of "one parent families" and was the touchstone for all future developments in welfare benefits to single parents of a kind that has made it financially more profitable to remain single than to marry.

---

[8] *Command Paper 5629 Report on July 2nd 1974*

Her book was reissued in 1992, shortly after it became known to journalists that her husband had been having an affair with another woman for seven years.

There are other agony aunts whose sermons are questionable but it would be too boring to continue a rather long list. It is obvious that leading by example has always been a feature of English life.

The reader may feel we have been going on for too long: but the point is this. There does not appear to exist in England (or as far as the present writer knows anywhere in the British Isles) any book which sets out to educate either in matters sexual or in marital happiness written by a broad-minded grandmother or grandfather, who may not have led a secluded life, with a few children, numerous grandchildren, happily married for many years, whose credentials in the relevant fields were incapable of being challenged. Why is it that in this country we are all told what to do by preachers whose sermons sound rather hollow?

Another factor that contributes to the somewhat uneven nature of sexuality in our country, especially relations between persons of the same sex, particularly males, is the public school system of education, about whose effects much has been said, especially by continental writers.

Given the statement of principle contained in the above Note, the topic will not be addressed any further here, suffice it however to observe that the first sexual experiences of any human being always leave a practically indelible psychological mark.

We should not overlook the impact of the sexual 'culture' which we have imbibed from our American cousins; not because they are more knowledgeable than we but mainly as a result of the indoctrination that the USA are imparting to the world and, more particularly, to Britain. This is made all the easier by the fact that we share what is said to be a common language; language apart, there is no doubt that 'things' generally start in the USA and end up in Britain...

If the unhealthy attitude to matters sexual resulting from the unbalanced and nonsensical education to which attention has already been drawn were to remain a personal problem, the situation might not be so bad. However, it is like a river in flood and it has now for a considerable amount of time (in fact, since the early 60s) burst its banks and has taken hold of our world of writing, filming and, most dangerously of all, public television. The descriptions and representations of twisted sexual activities are proffered with indecent regularity and crusading insistence, nay persistence, as though they were normal. There is a maniacal, diabolical approach said to be inspired avowedly by a desire (an excuse really) to educate and to clothe what is obviously aberrant in a framework of pseudo-scientific thought and imagery. A few examples will suffice.

To represent on television, as was done some time ago by Channel 5 a woman (?) having intercourse with a pig is not only indicative of the type of person that woman is but is the mark of a sick mentality, both on her part and on that of the producers of the programme, since a depiction of this kind cannot possibly be said to have either scientific or educational value and is projected solely to titillate. As recently as April 2008, in the course of a programme on BBC1 (a public network funded by taxpayers' licence fees) a woman was shown having 'intercourse' with a dog. A descent into hell?

There also have been on 'state' television, paid for by the public, representations of people drinking their own urine. What is the point of that?

Some years ago, one of the commercial television channels showed a group of people actually masturbating in public. Again, it is difficult to see the educational or scientific value of such a transmission.

It is worth mentioning that on Thursday 27th January 2000, in the course of a programme on British television (Channel 4), numerous representations were shown of the piercing of the clitoris with studs. Leaving aside practical considerations which are too obvious for words, one wonders about the sanity of the producers of such a show. A statement is attributed to Oscar Wilde to the effect that 'we are all lying in the gutter but some of us are looking at the stars'. Even assuming he was right, one is left to wonder, how in present-day England, we can quantify the 'some of us'...

Most damaging of all, however, is the fact that the forms of deviant sexual behaviour that are manifesting themselves, especially over the past 10/15 years, appear to be quite noticeable amongst our members of Parliament.

This is serious. In theory at least, our MPs are supposed to represent the people of England and, to some extent, to be almost the cream of the population. We are entitled to expect that they will behave honourably and in accordance with certain accepted standards of morality and propriety and, when caught out, at least to acknowledge their fault and go quietly: they seldom do... There is a very old Italian proverb to the effect that when a fish goes bad, it starts rotting at the head. On that basis, there is much that is rotten in our country and not merely in Hamlet's kingdom of Denmark.

A few examples, chosen at random, of the behaviour of some of our members of Parliament will suffice to provide flavour and support for the points being made here.

We had a Labour MP who picked up a rent boy with whom he had a rather long-standing affair. If that did not suffice, he employed him as a parliamentary researcher thus utilising taxpayers' funds to support his improper and illicit behaviour.

A Liberal Democrat MP, and married father of two, was found with two male prostitutes in a London flat committing a 'bizarre sex act too revolting to describe' for which act of humiliation he was paying more than £100. Bad enough, one might suppose; but it is somewhat difficult to decide whether to laugh or to be disgusted at the hypocrisy of the man who was publicly committed to family values.

A Conservative MP, when caught with his trousers down in a Midlands brothel that happened to have been raided by police and other officials, claimed that he was only there because whilst driving back home he got a stiff back and wanted a massage.

Another MP was caught having sex with a male on Clapham Common. More enjoyable, perhaps, is the fact that a member of the Welsh Assembly, when photographed in a sex act with another male at a location off the M4 motorway, claimed that he was there because of his interest in badger and bird watching.

Another MP posted pictures of himself in a state of semi-undress on the internet together with inviting sexual messages of an explicit nature.

The number of examples of this ilk is so great that it would become much too boring to list them all: they are indicative of the type of sexual deviation which is afflicting English society.

If, and it is a very big if indeed, the devil really exists, then Satan must be enjoying himself no end mixing with the English public, especially its MPs, TV managers and producers.

CHAPTER SIX – Few Apologies for the Wrong Sermons

The feminist writers who have come to the fore in the United States have all been closely followed in the United Kingdom and that is why it may be useful to add them to the list of "preachers"; all the more so because they had the decency to acknowledge that what they had initially advocated was wrong. A few examples will suffice, chosen not necessarily at random. The overall impact of feminism as a movement on our sexual customs is considered separately later; it suffices, for the moment, to identify the most vocal and "literary" personalities. Interestingly, perhaps, three of the women writers mentioned below were Jewish. It is a moot point whether any particular significance can or, indeed, should be attached to this fact. None is considered for present purposes and the occurrence may be pure coincidence.

At this point, one cannot resist the temptation of observing, of course, in passing, how worthless some of the grand declarations of principle by the more active feminists (who contributed to the building of the edifice of permissiveness whilst emasculated men looked on) appear to be when viewed over more than a couple of decades.

Recently (6 September 2000) we have seen the radical feminist Gloria Steinem (an American sociologist of Jewish extraction), the author of "Outrageous Acts and Everyday Rebellions", which paved the way for the 1970s movement and the inventor of the term "Ms" from the magazine she published by the same title, getting married to a South African; a man, of course, one presumes. It is said that she's on the record as having stated way back in 1983: "I will never get married; it is not an equal partnership. You lose your name, your credit rating, your legal residence, and socially you are treated as if his identity were yours".

She is also said to have remarked that it was pretty obvious that "some people have to pioneer being single". So much for consistency.

Furthermore, it is difficult to believe that her choice of marriage at age 66 can possibly have been prompted solely by a strong desire to have sexual comfort from a man. The more likely explanation is that she was affected by that fear of loneliness, which touches us all and becomes more marked as we get older. But why did she choose a man? Such a decision seems to contradict all her previous beliefs and is a clear warning to other feminists that they might be barking up the wrong tree when they maintain views which contradict nature. Sooner or later, nature will have its revenge.

One cannot help quoting at this stage the words of the well-known Latin poet, Horace: *"Naturam expellas furca, tamen usque recurret"*, usually translated into English as *"You may pitch nature out with a fork, she will soon come running back"*.

Gloria Steinem enjoyed in early times the co-operation of another activist in the feminist movement, Betty Friedan (she too an American sociologist of Jewish extraction), the author of "The Feminist Mystique", a seminal work in support of the feminist movement of the 60s and 70s. Both Steinem and Friedan viewed the family as the principal obstacle to the liberation of women and argued against its survival in today's world. In 1985, however, Betty Friedan began to have second thoughts and started making noises to the effect that maybe the family did have a role after all, which did not preclude the wife developing a separate identity. One cannot help wondering what view Betty Friedan takes of Steinem's marriage, particularly bearing in mind that when Friedan began to back-track, Steinem was most annoyed and refused to talk to her for 15 years.

It is also worth recording at this stage that Gloria Steinem is credited (see "The Times Book of Quotations", heading "Men and Women") with having said: *"A woman needs a man like a fish needs a bicycle."*

In a strange sense, there is no virtue, no moral and no religion in the modern feminist approach but merely a power-seeking exercise. As another writer, Andrea Dworkin, has observed[9] *"women manipulate men by manipulating men's sexual desire; these trivial, mediocre things (women) have real power over men through sex".* As a result *"for women, according to the killer/husband, virginity is the highest state, an ideal; and a fall from virginity is a fall into trivialisation, into being used as a thing……this reduction of humanity into being an object for sex carries with it the power to dominate men because men want the object and the sex".* {For the record, one should mention that Dworkin's book consists of nine chapters and has 191 pages of text. It is a classic display of modern feminist thinking and style: it is worth noting that the word "fuck" either as a verb or as a noun is used throughout the text 171 times. She clearly emerges victorious in her contest with "Lady Chatterley's Lover", for in D H Lawrence's book the words "fuck" or "fucking" appear a mere 30 times. Dworkin does not mention the word "love" once.}

---

[9] See Andrea Dworkin "Intercourse", Martin Secker and Warburg, London, 1987, Page 14

So much for America. On this side of the Atlantic, we had the Australian Germaine Greer actively pursuing the "rights" of women. Her major publication was "The Female Eunuch" in 1970. In it she wrote: "if women are to effect a significant amelioration in their conditions it seems obvious that they must refuse to marry". Here we go again... I suppose she now prefers to forget her 1970's contributions to the magazine "Oz" under the title "Cunt Power" – "Suck", as well as the text of 1969 by the title "Lady Love Your Cunt" (a sister magazine, in a sense, of the then infamous "Schoolkids".)

However, the author of this and other books seems to have mellowed as her hair has grown grey (she became 61 years old on January 30th, 2001). Whether it is because she has spent time in Italy, and has thus imbibed some of the Mediterranean, if not Catholic, spirit, or whether because she has begun to realise that any form of extremism is counterproductive, or more likely, that the feminist tenets for which she had so vigorously campaigned were and remain fundamentally flawed, it would be impertinent to say. Much time has, of course, passed since those days in the 70s when Germaine Greer was one of the driving forces behind the magazine Oz, the sister magazine of the then infamous Schoolkids publication, which was prosecuted under the Obscene Publications Act. Interviewed in early March 2010 on

English television and shown feeding peahens, she observed somewhat despondently that there had been change as a result of the “wars” between the sexes but “no revolution”.

Finally, it is difficult to resist the temptation of mentioning the changed attitudes of a fairly well-known radio personality in England. Another example of the vagaries of feminists’ consistent thought was displayed recently (July 2003) by a BBC Radio interviewer, well known amongst other things for the not-too-novel but always provocative statement that marriage makes slaves of women in favour of men. After 23 years of cohabitation with the father of her two children she decided to get married.

A highly vocal feminist, she had repeatedly argued that marriage humiliated women. In an interview reported in the Daily Mail of Saturday 12 July 2003 she said that her recanting was the result of inheritance tax, which is not payable on the death of a spouse. Strange what money will do for people. If her statement is true, it is probably easier to explain away in such a mercenary fashion the surrender of fundamental beliefs.

One supposes that the strength of the principle that marriage makes slaves of women could not have been that great, if it became overridden by venal considerations.

It is interesting to observe that most of these so-called educators have been of the female sex in recent times at least but what emerges from a careful analysis of their behaviour, if not of their writing, is that modern woman has been fairly inconsistent on major sexual issues.

More examples might serve to illustrate the point. The first one is very important, though long forgotten and practically unknown in England. In 1946 a courageous French woman, Madame Marthe Richard, a heroine of the French Resistance, in a desperate but ill-guided attempt to uphold the dignity of her sisters, campaigned vigorously and succeeded in having brothels closed throughout the country. The French registration system was ended and the so-called "houses of tolerance" were closed. A short while later, still in 1946, a card index system was established for contact tracing and the treatment of venereal disease, whilst in 1948 further legislation was passed restricting prostitution activities.

However, five years after her brilliant campaign to abolish brothels, Marthe Richard wrote a book called "L'Appel des Sexes". In it she acknowledged that she had been wrong; she accepted that brothels were necessary and pleaded that one should go back to the old system or, at the very least, that brothels should be allowed in the neighbourhood of Army camps. What caused her to change her mind was the accelerated and extravagant spread of venereal diseases after brothels were closed.

(Her crusading spirit was contagious and it spread to Italy where another woman, Angelina Merlin, achieved equal success in forcing the closure of brothels, although it took a little while longer in Italy, the official date of closure being February 20th, 1958.)

It is probably worthwhile underlining at this stage that most of the more recent feminist pronouncements, especially in the last three decades, have come from the United States of America. One would not wish to be too ungracious towards the most powerful nation on Earth, whose aid under the Marshall Plan gave a boost to defeated European countries after World War II, and whose contribution to modern history can in no way be underestimated. (Cynics will no doubt say that the Plan was inspired not so much by benevolence towards the defeated European nations but more by the desire to stop Russian expansion westwards; that is a different story.) But it is a sad fact of life that many of the evils that have affected humanity since 1492 have come to us from America.

A few instances of 'evils', which quite clearly originate on the other side of the Atlantic: tobacco, syphilis, the glorification of violence and of the profit motive, the unrestricted availability of divorce and, probably most importantly, exasperated feminism; wine lovers might also refer to the spread of 'oidium' and 'phylloxera' which decimated European vineyards.

Against this background, it is not surprising that we are somewhat confused about our sexuality. Of course, such confusion is not exclusive to England but is typical of the Anglo-American world generally and is shared by northern people like the Germans or the Scandinavians who view sex through rose-tinted glasses. Additionally, it is hardly a coincidence that romanticism, as a literary movement, started in England where confusion reigns about the nature and the roles of woman.

The uncertainty of feelings for woman is endorsed by English poets. It is not for a moment suggested that Thomas Gray's

"Elegy Written in a Country Churchyard" is to be blamed for the failure of the English people to understand their sexuality: that would certainly be inaccurate and over the top. But it should be stated unhesitatingly that the Englishman has problems in his assessment of woman and that his attitude towards her is, in most situations, completely ambivalent.

His approach to woman is very often inspired by what one can only term an unrealistically romantic view of her, which is the result of considerable naivety. Examples are legion, but what is probably a modern classic is the reference by a senior high court judge (Mr Justice Caulfield) to the middle-aged wife of a known public figure (the husband was subsequently, and in a different court, convicted of perjury) as "having fragance". Fragrant? Hardly the appropriate description to apply to any mature person of the female sex: vibrant maybe, fragrant no.

A statement of this kind reveals both a desire, if not a psychological need, to appreciate and, at the same time, a certain amount of ignorance. Some women, though not many, may undoubtedly be described as vibrant, none as fragrant. The only fragrance that can be associated with woman, unless she be a virgin both in body and in mind, is that resulting from a liberal application of perfume! But there speaks a cynic who, despite his possibly unkind view of the female sex, has been happily married to his one and only wife for more than 50 years, has three legitimate children and six grandchildren.

A further point to be made is that in England we appear to have developed ages ago at least one form of "sexual deviation" which has become specifically associated with the English: namely the use of violence, often extreme, whether self-inflicted or inflicted by others, with a sexual connotation. Round about 1800 the flagellation houses of the UK had become so famous that this particular kind of sexual practice was termed "The English Disease" ("Le Vice Anglais"). Evil wagging tongues even suggested that, when Crown Prince, George IV claimed that he had visited some of these places.

Not that there is anything unusual about flagellation anyhow. Common amongst the Asians, even Galen had thought that a modest amount of whipping toned the body. The use of leafy twigs is routine in Finnish, Russian and other hydrotherapy institutes and, as a matter of routine, has now been extended to most saunas in the western world. Nevertheless there is no doubt that flagellation has always been popular in England and one need only spare a few minutes looking at some of the advertisement cards that litter the principal UK cities (in telephone kiosks, newsagents, etc. etc.) to see that the majority of prostitutes still offer this kind of service and to an increasing extent. Services are not offered unless there is a demand for them and this particular form of advertising highlights the different approach of the American and the Anglo Saxon races to sexuality, thus confirming a practice that goes back even to the 17th Century. There is a reference to flagellation in Thomas Shadwell's (1642-1692) "The Virtuoso" – written in 1676 – and undoubtedly flagellating brothels were all the craze in the England during the 18th and 19th centuries. In them "governesses", as they were called (and indeed are still called today), administered the kind of pain for which the English have always been famous. The brothels of St James's in London were particularly numerous and much frequented.

The 'English vice' represents a factual and psychologically significant forerunner of the manifestations of sadomasochism, which have become so numerous nowadays, sometimes with fatal results.

The tendency towards sexual deviation in England knew no class, money or social distinction. Lord Melbourne, who was acquitted of charges of criminal conversation with Caroline Norton but abandoned her soon after his acquittal, was well known to indulge in flagellation in the 'bagnios' of St James's and elsewhere.

Everyone thought Lord Castleragh was a heterosexual with a keen interest in prostitutes but, just before he committed suicide, he is said to have dedicated some attention to a young boy. The poet Swinburne, undoubtedly as a result of the severe flogging received at Eton, is said to have enjoyed patronising No. 7 Circus Road in Regent's Park "a lovely little villa presided over by a well-educated lady well versed in the birchen mysteries"[10] and is known to have delighted in the flogging of young boys whom he described in his pornographic poems.

One cannot blame Palmerston for having endeavoured, as has been suggested, to force his attention upon one of Queen Victoria's ladies in waiting but when the police, in 1979, raided the premises of Cynthia Payne, who was running a brothel in south London, they found a Member of Parliament, a Lord and several Anglican priests, most of them in ladies' clothing, one dressed up as a waitress.

It is difficult to dispute the suggestion made by a number of foreigners that sexual "deviation" – whether in heterosexual or

---

[10] *A N Wilson "God's Funeral", John Murray, London 1999 page 209*

homosexual relationships or especially in misconduct with children – is typical of the English.

Such deviation is not only of long-standing but continues in the 21st century as the sexual revelations of the activities of an English 'icon' and many others have shown in 2012.

CHAPTER SEVEN – The Other Side of the Fence

So far one has concentrated on heterosexual activities. When it comes to the homosexual, there is probably less to say as concerns the amount of educational writing, because at least until the 20th century, not much was available to the general public. This is not to say that the practices did not exist both for men and for women. Indeed, they were quite common. For example, as early as 1727 in his "Gulliver's Travels" the Anglo-Irish satirist Jonathan Swift had remarked upon them. At the end of chapter seven of book four, he says in terms that love between persons of the same sex was quite common among the English.

Indeed, there is nothing novel about his observation. The extent of homosexual activity in Great Britain has always been fairly substantial no matter how well sheltered it may have been. Mediterranean and Arab people have always remarked upon this aspect of our sexual life and have commented that it can be extended to what one would term generally 'northern' countries (eg. Scandinavia and Germany) where homosexuality was over the centuries by no means an unusual activity.

In case the reader is wondering whether the extent of homosexual behaviour in Northern countries is a recent development, it is worth noting that way back in the second century the Greek grammarian Athenaeus (born in Egypt) wrote in one of his works that, perhaps somewhat surprisingly because their women were really beautiful, the Celts enjoyed the love of male youngsters far more than that of their women. So often, in fact, that some of them actually slept on animal skins with two young companions at the same time.

Until the 20th century, it is probably correct to say that sodomy was broadly condemned in the same manner as prostitution apart from being, theoretically at least, a criminal offence, whereas lesbianism seems not to have attracted the kind of attention that Radclyffe Hall provided for it. Of course, both kinds of sexual practices must have been around and they are certainly recorded, especially for central London where there were well-known cruising grounds, for instance, Lincoln's Inn Fields, the so-called "molly houses", the pubs, the taverns and the establishments which were known as meeting places for homosexuals. Indeed, this was a normal feature of English society and it was so even before the passing of liberalising legislation on this kind of male activity. A number of pubs existed in London in the 1950s, as well as nowadays, frequented almost exclusively by homosexuals in addition to many public lavatory facilities, one indeed in central Mayfair (in Three Kings' Yard, practically opposite the side entrance to Claridge's Hotel; it is now no longer there), where homosexuals congregated ("cottaging" being then, as now, a fairly common description).

Outside London probably there was less organised "plebeian" homosexuality although, given the set up of the country, opportunities could always be found at colleges, universities, inns of court, law courts, The public schools system, of course, lent itself.

The Kinsey Reports on males and females[11] found that 4% of American males were homosexuals. This figure was considered, even at that time, a gross underestimate but, more interestingly, the 1990 update of The Kinsey Reports finds that 25% of American males are wholly homosexuals; there do not appear to be similar up-to-date statistics for England.

The five English traitors of the 1950s Donald Maclean, Guy Burgess, Kim Philby, Anthony Blunt and Victor Rothschild, all from Cambridge, were homosexuals and passed on to the Russians details of both radar and atom bombs.

---

[11] *Philadelphia 1948 & 1953 W B Saunders Company*

Not too long ago there was an MP who was found "orange in mouth, oddly bedecked, hanging dead in his home"[12].

Another MP, accused of being on Clapham Common looking for homosexual encounters, claimed to have lost his way.

Looking back on the last hundred years or so, it is a little difficult to determine exactly how sexual customs in England have developed. Quite clearly, it seems to be the consensus that up to the Second World War most brides were virgins at marriage, but the matter goes further. A Channel 4 television programme in February 2002 recording the 1918 publication of the book "Married Love" by Marie Stopes claimed that "irregular sex or even no sex at all" was a feature of married life in England up to and including the Second World War. Young virgins were advised to lie back and think of England!

By the 1950s it was well known that Mediterranean youngsters (eager to escape from the reluctance of their girlfriends to have intercourse before marriage) who could afford to travel often claimed that they would come to England even in preference to Scandinavian countries because of the availability and willingness of the local girls.

---

[12] *Leo Abse "Fellatio Masochism Politics and Love", Robson Books, London 2000, p. 65*

However, it can be stated unhesitatingly that everything changed with the arrival of the contraceptive pill.

CHAPTER EIGHT – The Pill, a Sexual Hiroshima

Although in the United States they were quicker to take advantage of the work upon which Dr Pinkus had embarked in 1951 to discover whether progesterone could be taken with the deliberate purpose of controlling fertility, it was only in 1960 that the UK Medical Advisory Council and the Family Planning Association decided that it was safe to carry out larger scale trials than that previously set up in Puerto Rico for Enavid. As a result, over 1000 women in Birmingham, Slough and London, tried out the newly called Conovid pill, and a full report on these trials emerged in June 1961, endorsing both Conovid and an additional product called Anovlar, which were added to the list of approved oral contraceptives. But the Pill had commenced to be prescribed in the UK on 30 January 1961.

There is a poem by Philip Larkin (Annus Mirabilis) dated 16th June 1967, first appearing in "High windows" 1974 and reprinted in "Philip Larkin – Collected Poems"[13], the first strophe of which reads:

Sexual intercourse began in 1963
(which was rather late for me)
Between the end of the Chatterley ban
And the Beatles' first LP

---

[13] *The Marvell Press and Faber & Faber 1988 at page 167*

But perhaps Larkin got there late; others gained two years on him because the year 1961 was undoubtedly the one during which the contraceptive pill came of age in the UK and freely available. It was also the year that sounded the death knell for the early virginity of British young girls, and for that of other nationalities as well; but above all, there then began the gradual transfer of power from man to woman since it placed the female of the species in practically absolute control of the procreative cycle. Our indefatigable search for pleasure, as Freud called it, intensified.

What was not appreciated at the time, however, were the long-term effects of the introduction of the contraceptive pill. Only a few remarked on them. Amongst these must be mentioned one of the more forward-looking and liberal English judges, Lord Justice Scarman, who, in an address to law students, went on the record as saying that the long-term effects of the contraceptive pill would be much greater than those of the atom and hydrogen bombs. One is entitled to wonder whether in making such a forecast he also took into account that one of the most detrimental consequences of the introduction of the Pill was that it would inevitably give rise to the concept of political correctness. Political correctness, after all, is nothing but an extension of the concept of equality but taken to extremes which over the years have proved to be the most destructive element in the elimination of the principal virtue that has throughout the centuries inspired and protected this country, namely its common sense. It could be said that political correctness has resulted in the rape of common sense; one need hardly mention the absurdities which, combined with an idiotic and strict application of philosophical concepts of human rights and extreme health and safety requirements, it has brought about: absurdities and stupidities which are so evident and damaging in everyday life not only in England but also elsewhere in the world.

Incidentally, it is probably in keeping with our rather selfish social approach in the West that we have legislation about human rights but nowhere is there to be found a Human Duties Act... (or perhaps even a Human Values Act...).

Perhaps some keen do-gooder might wish to campaign for the passing of such an Act to remind us that there are no rights, in law as in practice, without corresponding duties; but be that as it may. The apparent disregard with which the 'great' British public has viewed and continues to view these two developments is puzzling.

Karl Marx was wont to observe that “religion is the opium of the peoples”; nowadays we ought to say that feminism and political correctness are the opium of British society and it is difficult to decide, no matter how objectively the situation is viewed, which of the two is more damaging.

It should be borne in mind that unfortunately any voice raised to object to such opiates would, in England at least, be in ‘falsetto’, or almost muted, as if the speaker were terrified that as a punishment a gutless government (we have had more than one!) might be tempted to bring back the death penalty.

Wrong. It could not: Strasbourg would see to that.

Flippancy apart, and on a much more serious note, the subdued tone of voice of those few well-intentioned people who might complain about the moral weaknesses of present-day English society bring to mind the image of the Roman Emperor Nero playing the fiddle whilst Rome was burning. But once more, enough preaching.

-------------------------------- o --------------------------------

It is hardly a coincidence that the decade was termed "the swinging sixties" since woman's inhibitions were swung right, left and centre. The liberalisation which occurred, considered at first shocking by a number of people, established itself so quickly that one cannot help wondering how strong some women's feelings of sexual repression and psychological enslavement must have been throughout the previous 2000 years.

The social and legal endorsement of the greater personal freedom in matters sexual, not only as regards heterosexual intercourse, but also in all other respects, occurred in 1960 when the prosecution brought against Penguin Books for publishing D H Lawrence's "Lady Chatterley's Lover" failed. It created an uproar.

Little did those who objected to the acquittal of the publishers realise how, compared to present day modern trash, "Lady Chatterley's Lover" could nowadays be considered almost a demure publication.

Women never looked back and in the 60s were very keen to sacrifice their virginity at an early age. It is true that some have subsequently gone on the record, both in print and on television, as saying that a mistake was made; but the fact remains that from the 60s onwards a virgin woman was a commodity which man would find increasingly scarce at marriage, as already observed.

With respect to the Gospels (Matthew 19:24, Mark 10:25 and Luke 18:25) one may now say that it is easier for a camel to pass through the eye of a needle than to find a virgin at the altar (more about virginity in a later chapter).

Most damagingly, however, the Pill has resulted in a normal definition of intercourse divorced from its basic function of procreation, so that it is now much clearer to youngsters and at much earlier ages that they can have "fun" without running any risk of being held accountable for pregnancies, without having to worry too much except about AIDS, and without any form of commitment being engendered.

Statistics published in July 2011 maintain that the number of STIs – sexually transmitted infections – (previously known as STDs – sexually transmitted diseases) in the UK exceeds half a million new cases each year with a substantial cost to the National Health budget.

Politicians and sociologists raise their arms in despair and surprise when they have to confront the regrettably true protests, by women, that men are cads and incapable of accepting responsibility. However, they prefer to ignore completely that this reluctance or inability, disgraceful though it is, on the part of modern males, to accept responsibility for anything when it comes to relationships with women, is the result of a substantial depreciation in the significance of intercourse.

From the standpoint of the male, the argument runs that if the woman wanted equality, she's got it, and if she wanted fun, she's had it too (one hopes!), so why should he bother about the consequences? The attitude of woman is just as much affected, but in a totally different sense. Deep down, because her primary function of motherhood is still there, her instincts tell her that she should be able to elicit commitment from her sexual partner but modern influences are such that she is concerned about the possible "subjection" that this approach would entail. In other words, modern woman wants to keep her cake and to have eaten it at the same time.

The freedom from the risk of pregnancy inevitably encouraged promiscuity, though the availability of the Pill in itself was aimed simply at avoiding the result of intercourse. There is a long-standing argument that the traditional unwillingness of women in the main from Latin and/or Catholic countries to surrender their virginity until marriage was not the result of a generally held religious belief but merely the fear that the girl might get pregnant. This argument is not to be discounted lightly, of course, but whether it be right or wrong an aura of intactness of women while still young was created in society: that has now gone and with it, some writers have suggested, young women's coyness and modesty.

This may or may not be a fact but what is to be recorded is the opinion of certain modern psychologists that the thoughts of young women have become increasingly lascivious. Whether such lasciviousness also leads modern young English women into drunkenness and drug taking is a much more speculative matter. On the other hand, English (and for that matter, American) women seem to have become more... pious. It is somewhat difficult to refrain from observing that if films and TV programmes are to be believed, English speaking women tend to become religious in intercourse.

More and more common are the representations of orgasm accompanied by repeated saying of 'oh my god'. Is it the result of surprise or religious belief? Difficult to say, since statistical information is obviously lacking.

It would appear, however, that this is exclusively an American/English reaction since enquiries have shown that French women in similar circumstances don't say 'mon dieu' any more than Italian women might say 'mio dio' or even perhaps 'o dio mio' or German 'mein gott' or even Spanish women 'o dios mio'.

One feature that marks out modern English women is their relaxed approach to sexual intercourse. Perhaps relaxed is not the right word since there is casualness about their approach to sex, which is somewhat worrying.

It is as though the giving of oneself is no different from having a shampoo. Gone is the concept that there is a time and place for everything, as witness the newspaper reports, on a daily basis, of behaviour, which our grandmothers would have been horrified at hearing about, if not ashamed to relate, even assuming that they were aware of its significance. There were published on November 17th 2010 statistics to show that 48% of women between the ages of 20 and 30 admitted to having indulged in intercourse on what are euphemistically described as "one-night-stands". Intercourse with a complete stranger. One can't help wondering whether they were actually standing up or lying down?

A noticeable trait of how sexual activity manifests itself amongst English women, especially the younger ones, is in fact the promptness with which they indulge in intercourse with men they hardly know. Even leaving on one side the so-called one-night stands, the youngster nowadays no longer expects to have to wait for his girlfriend's favours. Immediacy replaces familiarity, courtship has become non-existent, wooing is a thing of the past.

Girls cooperate in the taking of short cuts to intercourse; boys no longer enjoy the excitement and pleasure of the hunt. Indeed, one might suggest that the resultant lack of excitability is a prime factor in reducing their erectility; but that is a separate argument (picked up later).

One would think that women might prefer at least to appear to put up some resistance before being 'conquered', to enjoy the satisfaction of catching the male in their webs; but that seems no longer required. Gone is the coyness, the apparent disinterest, the helplessness, indeed the artfulness with which women have always entrapped their prey: in short, the fun has gone out of it!

Statistics are, of course, quite often unreliable but the above percentage is so high as to be a cause for concern, at least as far as the probability of the spread of venereal disease. But the matter does not stop there. Many of these precocious young girls do not even bother to have protected sex, about which they are so to say brainwashed when at school during sex lessons, where they are taught how to place a condom on an erect penis (plastic, one hopes...) as if that particular exercise required a great deal of teaching. But they don't seem to bother about applying that knowledge in practice, if the rate of illegitimacy is anything to go by.

They embark upon intercourse in a strange sense keeping their fingers crossed that they will neither get pregnant nor catch any form of sexually transmitted disease, let alone Aids. A cynic might remark that they would do a lot better to keep their legs crossed.

When interviewed, many youngsters maintain that there is little benefit in the sex education courses arguing that much more is to be learned about sexual activity by the present ever-increasing trend to what is known as sexting, namely the communication, via mobile telephone, images of nudity and often more than that. Their main complaint seems to be that the imparting of general notions about reproduction, sex organs and related matters is too mechanical and what is neglected, most of the time, are the emotions and the long-term effects of sexual activity.

One can state with confidence that the UK has now become the single parent capital of Europe. Statistics show that the proportion of women aged 18-35 who are single mothers is getting close to ten percent. This is to be compared with a rate approximating one percent in Spain, and 0.5 percent in Italy. But let's leave statistics on one side and concentrate on English young girls.

We should not forget that over the centuries we have, despite outward appearances, been overall inclined to bawdy and drunken behaviour. For example, in 19th Century England there was indiscriminate sexual activity coupled with or resulting from a heavy drinking culture of the kind so accurately and significantly depicted by Hogarth in his drawings and cartoons. Taverns, pubs and retailers of beer abounded especially after the Beer Act 1830 was passed. The result of this Act was the deregulation of sales of beer throughout the country so cheap drink was available for all, especially beer and gin (Mother's Ruin). In a sense we can find an equivalent in today's situation where the drinking culture continues unabated despite all Government efforts, helped in particular by the reduced price of alcohol especially in supermarkets.

One reads about the various temperance campaigns and the incentive to sign 'the Pledge'. But these had only marginal effects, which were short term. Excessive drinking is, generally speaking, the mark of northern people (Germans, Scandinavians and British, of course). It is proving difficult to eradicate in our country and, although not strictly relevant to the theme of this work, it is probably worthwhile drawing the attention of the reader that on the 28th November 2012 the Home Office published figures to show that the cost to the nation of alcohol abuse was calculated at £41 billion.

In drinking customs as in sexual licence the English factual and above all psychological heritage is a causative element in the development of a sexual culture which is inevitably unbalanced.

On a different level, present-day hooligans do no more than what our ancestors used to do; it is almost as though there is a regression to centuries past, as if something was already there, in the genes, and has resurfaced in more favourable conditions brought about by liberalising attitudes. Whether such attitudes are the result of the availability of the Pill, or greater 'laissez-faire' or political correctness one can debate for a very long time. The debate would almost be sterile because the reactions of a people can never be taken in isolation from their history and their surroundings.

In England women were kept in a state of submission throughout the 18th and 19th centuries. They have now come into their own. There is no way in which the clock can be put back.

CHAPTER NINE – The Virgin Bride, a Needle in the Haystack

The availability of the contraceptive pill compounded this very phenomenon of the willingness of young girls to embark on sexual activity at an increasingly early date and without establishing any kind of lasting emotional relationship: it is worthy of closer attention. Sexual education in schools "aggravated" the situation so that there now appears to be a pattern of behaviour by young girls, which highlights a confusion about life that is becoming much more obvious and increasingly dangerous to society as time passes.

The depreciation of virginity should not be too easily discounted. A number of reasons are given for this, for example that religious beliefs, both in the Protestant and the Catholic world, have become less significant nowadays; alternatively that girls mature at a much earlier age (11 or 12 years). One thing is certain: namely that the average age of first intercourse in the UK has gradually dropped from 21, as it was in the 1970s, to 17 as in the 1990s, and now stands at 14/15.

(A National Health Service Report published on December 16th 2011 records the fact that more than a quarter of English girls lost their virginity below the legal age of consent, as well as mentioning that one in eight girls below the age of 15 had already had more than ten sexual partners. Whilst it is true that any kind of information of this nature is to be taken with more than a pinch of salt, there must be some foundation and evidence for the statements being recorded by the NHS.)

There will inevitably have to be sooner or later a debate as to whether the reduction in the age of first intercourse is the result of a relaxation of socio/sexual restraints or a direct consequence of what is now being diagnosed as precocious puberty. This author is not qualified to comment on that particular aspect of the matter save to observe that one can reach puberty at 11 and still refrain from having intercourse until a much later date.

The previous generations' concern about virginity did not last too long; but there is no doubt that youngsters of today would fail to understand how women of yesteryear were very well protected, especially in the Victorian era when they had chaperones and their contacts with males were not encouraged.

An aura of bigotry prevailed especially when it came to extramarital affairs and theatrical performances and up to the second part of the 20th century it was believed that woman's essential duty was to get married and have children. If and in so far as she intended to give herself pleasure in marriage and to enjoy sex in the same way as men did, this was exclusively through the act of copulation.

Everything was done in the 19th century hypocritically to control sexuality. For example, as regards public performances, the Lord Chamberlain, who was controller of what was or was not permitted (as obscene) in the theatre, ruled like a despot. Plays had to be submitted before they could be performed and when he thought fit, he would ensure that changes of dialogue and characterisation were made before a play could be performed in public. It is a fact that even a fairly elementary book on birth control ("The Wife's Handbook") resulted in its doctor authors being struck off by the General Medical Council.

In the 1920s and 30s there was a very well known and often disliked Home Secretary, Joynson Hicks, who was particularly severe and for that reason was much satirised for his efforts to control sexual activity by upholding 'old principles'.

The Director of Public Prosecutions, Sir Archibald Bodkin, was no less keen to prosecute so-called obscene books and plays, which were thought to offend Christian sexual mores and public taste.

Up to the 1960s sex remained tied to marriage but, with increasing divorce, sexual activity swung free. The result was what J B Priestly termed 'hypocrisy of self-deception' especially concerning homosexual activity between consenting adults, which had been a criminal offence since 1885.

It was not until 1968 that the Office of the Lord Chamberlain was abolished.

But a desperate search for sexual freedom and greater satisfaction both for men and women started soon after World War II. The British public went through a number of phases at different times with varying solutions and unexpectedly novel techniques being proposed by writers, doctors, agony aunts and feminists.

There were many of each such counsellors!

Their aims seemed to be concerned primarily with the mechanical aspect of sex rather than with the emotional. There was almost a pathological insistence on the primary importance of female orgasm; there then followed woman's freedom of choice since the theory was that by these two means – the achievement of orgasm and the freedom to choose – woman's social and personal status would improve.

The first step towards such improvement was the creation of the Pill, which has already been dealt with.

The second step was taken when it was decided in 1969 by the Divorce Reform Act that marriage was not the panacea for male/female satisfaction. Reaching such decision was made all the easier, of course, by the availability of the contraceptive pill which dissolved the time-honoured tie between reproduction and sex. Once the fear of pregnancy was eliminated it was inevitable that one should concentrate on sex education, which became an essential feature.

What easily and almost logically followed from this was the idea that sex was not primarily for reproduction but essentially for fulfilment and pleasure. Nevertheless, problems did arise since most women were not, and still are not, the sexual athletes that sex pundits and sociologists of the 70s assumed they would become through education.

Most of our sexual teachers ignored, or maybe had forgotten, a fundamental need of woman, namely that 'sexual' pleasure not only means a strenuous and constant physical effort but, much more importantly, emotional feelings of closeness and tenderness. But let us continue.

From this it was easy to argue that it was right and proper to 'discover' and as a result to glorify woman's ability to have multiple orgasms. Though it was not admitted this was, of course, not really a great discovery but it was not realised that it would be a dangerous one to underline and encourage because it raised the average woman's performance in bed to pinnacles, which are precluded in any event to many women and the achievement of which presupposes the collaboration of a man capable of great penile power, much sensitivity, mature understanding and, for a man, incredible unselfishness.

A consequence of this realisation dawning that the number of such men was limited was the insistence on a recourse to masturbation on the part of woman.

Gradually through the 70s and 80s the idea that woman was at last 'mistress of her own body' resulted in her being freer to have affairs despite being married. Spontaneity of instinct became more important than marital loyalty, so much so that certain calculations put the rate of adultery by UK married women during marriage to as high as approximately 70%: hopefully, an over-estimate!

The inevitable consequence of this development was a downgrading of monogamy, which was sacrificed on the altar of individual unrestrained choice. Where, however, there remained some psychological reluctance to slaughter the innocence of a lifelong relationship, people began to argue for a so-called 'open' marriage where candour (euphemistically) replaced fulltime commitment and unbridled passions overrode marital chastity. The concept of 'wife-swapping', which had been so popular in the 70s having gradually dwindled, little was left for enterprising, dissatisfied spouses but to resort to the psychiatrist's couch!

The number of women and, to a lesser degree, men in need of treatment required an alternative, namely cohabitation, which soon became, and has remained, the norm as the best way to retain some form of clarity of conscience and, endorsed by law and by financial resources, woman's decision to do her own thing.

The added bonus was the increasing respectability of cohabitation, the expression 'living in sin' losing completely its meaning and, above all, its currency.

The net result was that the retention of virginity prior to marriage ceased to have any significance as marriage itself lost its sense of novelty and of celebration. The bride's white dress is still with us, of course, but the once factual and nowadays only notional purity of the woman at marriage went quite easily and almost unnoticed out of the window.

CHAPTER TEN – Woman in Command

The trouble nowadays, which clearly was not foreseen when cohabitation was endowed with respectability, is that especially after long periods of living together when cohabiting parties separate, particularly when there are children, the problems engendered by separations and the consequent legal difficulties have become in 2012 almost as great, if not greater, than those generated by divorce. Whilst this is a boon for lawyers and social workers, it is a clog on the legal system and an additional burden for the children involved to have to bear.

As already underlined above the result of the introduction of the contraceptive pill was that by 1964, London had acquired the tag of being a swinging place where mini-skirted women walked about flaunting their sexuality.

It was left to Masters and Johnson's "Human Sexual Response" way back in 1966 to glorify clitoral enjoyment thus compensating for the anxiety felt by those women who otherwise might consider themselves frigid. Quite clearly, and rightly, the argument was that foreplay makes intercourse more pleasant, although it had been appreciated for centuries that the clitoris was an essential part of woman's sexual enjoyment and voluptuousness.

By the end of the second millennium clitoral enjoyment had become a mantra and little if no attention was paid to the idea that there are some women whose religious beliefs prevent them, at least in theory, from masturbating or who prefer or at least have been educated to enjoy vaginal pleasure, rather than clitoral, nor to the fact that for those millions of women throughout the world who have undergone clitoridectomies, clitoral enjoyment simply doesn't exist. One is entitled to ask rhetorically whether such women do not enjoy sexual relations for that reason or whether in fact they should be treated as lesser creatures.

(I leave to others the debate as to which of the two types of enjoyment a woman really prefers save to observe that inevitably, during intercourse, both have a part to play.)

Given that by the mid-60s the prevailing view was that sex was not so important because one of its results was the giving of life but much more because of the satisfaction that it provided, it was inevitable that there should occur a downgrading of the child-bearing function.

The obvious result of this was the passing in 1967 of the Abortion Act which gave women a decisive role in determining whether it was to be man or woman who had the responsibility of carrying on the species. Whilst the further step towards woman choosing what kind of sexual life she wished to have took a little more time to become evident, it was not too long delayed.

At the same time, as it became current thinking that sexual relations were not aimed primarily at procreation but rather at enjoyment, it did not take too long to decide that homosexual activities were just as 'respectable' as heterosexual ones.

One cannot help remarking about the present extensive existence and availability of lesbian activity coupled with the amount of writing about it especially during the latter part of the 20th century.

Until the 1920s the amount of literature relating to female heterosexuality was reasonably limited. This is understandable because given the greater social and political importance of man as distinct from woman, it was of greater interest to society to know which persons of the male sex had homosexual relations because of the probable impact on their social and political behaviour. Female heterosexuality was much less important and therefore lent itself very little to the written word.

Vita Sackville-West wrote of her awakening to a different kind of sexual desire, as is well known. One wonders, however, whether her lesbianism would have remained dormant if she had been married to a different kind of man rather than Harold Nicolson (from whom she had two children) who was known for his homosexuality. In fact, they had what is known as an open marriage so she could indulge her leanings; it was rumoured that she had more than 50 lesbian lovers – including Virginia Woolf, Dora Carrington and Violet Trefusis – despite her trying (or so it is said) to be discreet. The same discretion cannot be ascribed to Radclyffe Hall who had to go into print in "The Well of Loneliness" which was duly published in 1928. How almost innocent and demure were all those flings of the '20s compared to what has happened in the UK since the '60s when much greater openness has simplified behaviour. If homosexual men could be allowed to 'come out' and boast about their tendencies, why should not women? Rather like a staircase up to a heaven for woman or, depending on one's point of view, down to a hell for men. Or perhaps, as modern thinking goes, neither: purely a long-delayed liberalisation of sexual customs in a free-for-all mood and a more sophisticated expression of female sexuality.

Lesbianism would soon become fashionable, of course. People tend to forget that it has always existed, though the Victorians had refused to acknowledge it believing it to be preferable that young immature girls should remain untouched by lewd non-heterosexual thoughts. That at least was the public stance; privately, the matter stood otherwise.

Once the clitoris was glorified the extent of lesbianism became more noticeable and it was now possible to maintain that women were mature also when they only achieved clitoral orgasm.

Are modern English women any happier as a result? It is obviously not for a man to jump to conclusions on this issue save to observe that modern women are much more anxious than their grandmothers. Whilst sex is no longer a taboo subject there seems still to be an element of perhaps guilt, certainly shame as far as English women are concerned. This arises mainly from the fact that with the disappearance of courtship any heterosexual act seems inspired rather than by love, by technique. There is a constant concern about living up to certain standards, which are not generally speaking available to the majority of human beings.

This point has already been made but it needs repeating, since it is often maintained with some degree of truth that only 10% of men can really satisfy a woman!

What the long-term effects of this early commencement of sexual activity will be, both on woman's reproductive cycle, on her general health, and, indeed, on her sexual desire in more mature years, must remain a matter for speculation.

Who knows? What we do know however is that there is very little that is angelic about the modern attitude to sex in the UK. A study published by the title "Sexual Behaviour in Britain" (December 2001) shows beyond any doubt that the sexual experiences of youngsters in the UK are not satisfactory. Girls will surrender themselves in all likelihood to conform to the expectation of their peers and the "mores" of our society. Given the present type of behaviour, it is not too far-fetched to say that there is a good chance that the girl might be half or totally drunk on either alcohol or drugs and the same may well be true of the boys.

Anyone who is in doubt as to the validity of the statement that has just been recorded should look at Table 2.13 p.76 of the study of "Sexual Behaviour in Britain" where the percentages of men and women who claim that they were drunk when they had intercourse is respectively is 63.2 and 64.2, which coupled with the exceptionally high percentage recorded by women (67.6) in respect of first intercourse, namely that they had *"just met for the first time"* their partner, is a strong enough commentary on present-day attitudes. The same table shows that as a causative element in first intercourse love figured only at 31.2%, prompting the authors of the report to record (p.77) that *"there is little evidence of any return to an age of romanticism, certainly among women".* Interestingly (p.79) "younger respondents are more likely than older ones to report having been a 'bit drunk' at first intercourse".

And finally, in this context, more than half (58.5%) women who had first intercourse under the age of 16 went on the record to say that they thought it was too soon. Quite naturally, boys looked at it differently. The report's only comment of any significance is to say that *"it is uncommon, and increasingly so, for first sexual intercourse to take place within marriage".*

This factor cannot be taken in isolation from the raising of so-called sex education, almost to a curriculum subject, in schools. It must be a matter of common sense that the early teaching of sex encourages earlier experimentation. If you are taught to be a surgeon, you will wish to operate. By parity of reasoning, without wishing in any way to run down the imparting of any kind of knowledge in a free society, it must follow as night day, that youngsters who receive sex education, will start experimenting at a much earlier date than they otherwise would. For the record, since October 23rd 2010 to date, sex and relationships (whatever the latter now may mean) education is compulsory in England. It is worthwhile to remind ourselves of a statement way back in 1973 by a Birmingham headmaster, Roger Probert, that "all teaching in all subjects aims to stimulate interest. It would be odd if this were not true of sex lessons".

(We might consider introducing exams in sexuality, perhaps with practical performances!).

This is not the place to examine the benefits of sex education as compared with the blissfulness of ignorance. Suffice it to observe that the number of teenage pregnancies in Great Britain has risen consistently since the 50s. The relevant figures have been quoted earlier on and will be referred to again. One cannot, however, fail to remind the reader that it is now being reported that English youngsters (males and females) have the highest incidence in Europe of sexually transmitted infections. One of the results is the reduced effectiveness of established medication in curing such infections, especially gonorrhoea. Nowadays, the waiting rooms of most UK surgeries advertise the fact that tests for Chlamydia are available free of charge.

A cynic might be forgiven for observing that we have taught our youngsters very little indeed. One is discounting completely for present purposes the argument that there seems to be little point in teaching "the facts of life" divorced from any moral, spiritual and social guidance about the consequences of giving effect to such teaching. Indoctrination and education are not coincident.

One cannot refrain at this stage from observing that whilst the aseptic imparting of sexual education should at least theoretically be conducive to a greater sense of responsibility in human relations, it has a drawback, which is not often commented upon: namely its highly damaging effect in depriving the youngsters of the use of their imagination. This is a common failing of Western society because the impact of television and other means of mass communication make it very difficult to use our imagination. Unfortunately, as the French writer Maupassant had observed in 1898 in one of his short stories, 'the more you lift the veil of the unknown, the more you reduce the imagination of both men and women'. True: but the veil is being lifted, amongst other forms, by means of communications such as Twitter where no standard is applied as to the accuracy and the quality of the bulk of comments and information which are provided.

There is ample justification for the description of the decade 1960-1970 as the 'Swinging Sixties'. From an historical point of view there is no doubt that as far as the UK is concerned there then occurred a turning point for British society in the 12 years from 1959 to 1971.

They saw in sequence the Obscene Publication Act 1959, which, to some extent, albeit a limited and hypocritical one, relaxed English law on obscenity.

Practically at the same time the Street Offences Act was passed that same year – consequent on the recommendations of the Wolfenden Committee – in an attempt – which quite clearly has failed – to drive prostitutes off the streets; then we had the shock provided by the nude photographs of the Duchess of Argyle divorce case; the Profumo affair with Christine Keeler; the almost incredible success of the 'Carry On' type of films, which projected onto the large screen much that could not be published; the all-important development of printed photographic pornography, the magazine 'Penthouse' being founded in the USA in 1965 by Bob Guccione (who somewhat later – see Channel 4 TV, 4th October 2001 – organised the 'Great American Pissing Contest' for women: how elegant); the Family Planning Act 1967, which provided unlimited contraception; the

Abortion Act of that same year sponsored by David Steele; the abolition of theatre censorship in 1968 with the concomitant open display of nudity and vulgarity on stage; the introduction of basic sex education in schools in 1969; the opening of the first sex supermarket by Ann Summers in 1971; what was to become a true British mania for the music of The Beatles and the films of James Bond and, above all, in 1969 the Divorce Reform Act, which made available for the first time divorce on demand. In fact, it can be stated unhesitatingly that, as a result of that piece of legislation, divorce in the UK has become a free-for-all because not only is it childishly easy to obtain but also because the relevant proceedings, nowadays much simplified, are at present quite inexpensive. Indeed, one can now divorce on the internet.

This is probably an inevitable development in the sense that just as the marriage ceremony has lost all its significance, so has marriage itself.

If one considers that the package tour industry (that made travelling for sun and sex a much desired development, which continued for decades as being extremely popular) started in 1971, one can realise how, in just over a decade, the moral and social face of England was altered dramatically.

The failure of the prosecution of D H Lawrence's *Lady Chatterley's Lover* has already been referred to above.

Women (and men) never looked back. The question arises however whether some of the consequences of this so-called liberalisation are damaging not only to the individuals but above all also to society. One of the most unfortunate results is the increase in the number of illegitimate births to underage girls and the increased figure for the number of abortions rising to more than 250,000 in 2011.

(I hope not to become too boring but I should warn the reader that I shall have to refer again, from time to time, to official information and statistical data. This is perhaps annoying but I am afraid it is essential to focus the mind on the enormity and gravity of the distortions and, indeed, corruptions of our sexual behaviour.)

It certainly cannot be said that there is lack of knowledge about human sexual activity. Starting with the Kinsey Reports (1948 on men and 1954 on women) and continuing with the number of publications that have followed upon them, the transformation of sex, which the Kinsey Reports are said to have provoked, has had some rather unexpected consequences. In the journal of the

American Medicine Association, there was published on February 11th, 1999 a study by Dr Edward Laumann, which suggests that America's so-called vast culture of sexual fantasy is as remote from reality as we are from the Martians.

The survey was based on 90-minute interviews with 1749 women and 1410 men, concentrating in particular on women in the age group 18-29. Of these 26% said that they regularly failed to achieve orgasm, 27% said that sex brought them no real pleasure and 32% went so far as to maintain that sex did not even interest them.

43% of women felt pain, anxiety or conspicuous lack of pleasure during sexual intercourse and at least 30% of men have a number of problems ranging from premature ejaculation to inadequate or non-existent erections.

The impact of America in all its manifestations upon British society is too well known to require discussion here. Dr Laumann's study is indicative of a general malaise.

It is discomforting to read on July 23rd 2010 the conclusions of an English study of some 4,300 young women. The main findings were that one fifth of girls under 18 had been pregnant, 83% had lost their virginity by 18 and 27% of those before 16, 18% have had miscarriages and 1,300 had been pregnant at least three times before the age 18.

Figures have emerged recently (18th April and 28th April 2011) that highlight the state of English society. They are very worrying indeed and endorse the fact that traditional family life in England is on the verge of collapse.

The report by the Organisation for Economic Co-operation and Development (better known as the OECD) makes depressing reading.

After Denmark (58%) the United Kingdom has the highest percentage (50%) of mothers working when the child is 12 months old. The government seems neglectful of the fact that children who are 'abandoned' by their mother before a certain age have a greater chance of bad behaviour, coupled with poor literacy and scholastic performance.

Recent statistics (2nd November 2012) are perhaps even more shocking since they show that only half of 15-year-olds now live with both parents.

Dealing with divorce, the report shows that 63% of the total divorces in the UK occur where couples have children, the impact of divorce being detrimental to those children. Furthermore statistics published in May 2012, indicate that one in 11 couples splits up before a child of the marriage is five years old.

The report also points out the oddity that in financial terms British single parents get the sixth best incentives in Europe, whilst married couples get the tenth worst.

It appears that births outside marriage are at their highest level for 200 years. 50% of children can now expect their parents to separate or divorce by the time they reach the age of 16.

Cohabitation before marriage has now become the norm since nine out of ten married couples have so lived. Before the Second World War, fewer than one couple in 30 cohabited. Indeed, marriage is becoming less and less either undertaken or helped by successive governments and it has now been determined that more couples cohabit than get married.

The stigma attached to women who had children outside wedlock has disappeared completely.

It has been found that just under 50% of children born in England are born to unmarried mothers. Not for the first time, the disadvantages of a child born in a one-parent set-up are underscored since it is recorded that about 75% of such children are more likely to fail scholastically, about the same number are more likely to become addicted to drugs, 50% are more likely to have problems with alcohol, as indeed any assistant whether medically qualified or not in casualty departments throughout the country would be able to confirm and 35% are more likely to be unemployable as adults.

Statistics of such detrimental though hardly surprising character continue to emerge coincidentally with the irresponsible ignoring, where it does not amount to denigration, of “traditional” values.

Against such a background it must have come as little surprise to the ‘great’ British public to learn on the 6th June 2011 that England comes 17th amongst European nations in the care it dedicates to its elderly people. In this league table, we spent 5.8% of our GDP whereas the two top countries, Italy and France, spent respectively 11.7% and 11.1%. The short-sightedness of our society is extreme, surely, when people forget that one day they too may be in need of better care as they grow old.

A further item of news may be relevant. It was reported on May 25th 2011 that in 2010 there were over 20,000 abortions carried out on women under 25 years of age who had already undergone one or more abortion interventions.

A few more statistical items which highlight the parlous state of sexual/social relations in England: there are close to two million single mothers having one or more children and three million children live in households where there is only one parent[14]; every year half a million children and adults are drawn into the legal system; at the moment 3.8 million children are currently caught up in family litigation.

Research by the Youth Justice Board claims that 70% of young offenders come from broken homes.

Nor should one ignore the financial cost to society of all these family and divorce related problems, which is far from negligible and which is estimated at £44 billion a year (as at May 1st 2012).

It is difficult to refrain from observing that these young women either were not paying much attention at school during sex education classes (which is unlikely, given the keen interest of

---

[14] *Office for National Statistics, January 2012*

youngsters in matters sexual) or – which is more likely – were probably drunk and/or drugged and did not have sufficient good sense to take contraceptive precautions when 'having fun'.

It is obviously true that, perhaps deservedly, Britannia no longer rules the waves, but one thing appears beyond dispute if the statistical data provided herein is correct, namely that Britannia undoubtedly rules the waves of moral incontinence.

The figures quoted are indicative of a malaise that is affecting us all in the UK. It is like a tsunami which sweeps away all concepts of dignity and, dare I say it, morality, which have served our country in good stead. What is somewhat hard to follow is the passive way in which we are reacting to it. The truth is that we are no longer surprised by these excesses; indeed, we take them for granted as an ordinary feature of social life in the 21st century.

When information of the nature indicated above emerges together with salacious descriptions of the concomitant and causative behaviour, we almost shrug our shoulders. We are not bothered by what we see on television or read in the press. In fact, one could say we almost expect nothing different.

It is as though most of us have taken a policy decision to avert our glances from behaviour and statistics in respect of which we still feel a scintilla of disapproval, but are reluctant to voice any form of dissent. A similitude that springs to mind is the acceptance of absurd representations of blobs of paint on a canvas as art: not too many people have the self respect and courage to describe some aspects of modern art as what it really is, namely the impertinent and regrettably successful attempt to take the general public for a ride.

No better example of this typically English tendency to avert one's glances from particular kinds of sexual activity by certain people can be found than the recent events concerning questionable conduct by a public figure over a period of more than 40 years.

It is sometimes suggested (by way of comment, of course, and never of criticism) that behaviour which gives rise to the emergence of figures such as those quoted above is either youthful exuberance or assertion of individual rights: this is a view that is cultivated by more than one section of our society and is now becoming almost prevalent in modern Britain. Indeed, one is reminded of the saying: 'if you can't beat them, join them'.

Whilst such an attitude is undoubtedly useful if one wishes to climb the staircase of social improvement and public recognition, or at least acknowledgement, it is no guide to an individual's rule of life, for it puts paid to any form of integrity of belief and behaviour.

Furthermore, some of the writing in the Anglo-American 'language' about sexual relationships generally is not only negative but also highly suspect. There is a concentration on the power balance between men and women, which appears to ignore the realities of sexual life, as the quotation transcribed above of the words of Mary Wollstonecraft and Andrea Dworkin shows beyond a shadow of a doubt.

Additionally, we are becoming increasingly short-sighted in our thinking also because it is much easier supinely to accept uncritically that societies and sexual behaviour must change through the generations. It is, of course, true that the older generation has a different perception of relations between the sexes than that prevailing at the moment. In the same vein, it is also true that the elders in one generation do not usually understand and too often criticise the behaviour of their younger contemporaries. Despite all this, the world continues to exist, we all survive, some of us may even be better off and healthier than our parents: so, why bother? It will sort itself out, it normally does.

This is an argument that is often heard and is repeated whenever one complains about matters. It is, of course, a perfectly plausible theory to maintain that we shouldn't really bother because life goes on; things merely change. But what this approach doesn't take into account is the harm that is done by not acknowledging that some of the changes are highly damaging to the individual's mental if not physical health and to the well-being of society as a whole. But perhaps, again, one is moralising...

It is troublesome to note the ever-increasing concern of woman to assert her dominance over man, resulting in a deterioration in the significance of heterosexual intercourse which, for many women, is the last vestige of their subjection to man. These desperate attempts at 'domination' explain the woman's frequent assumption of a dominating position in intercourse since the traditional posture places her below the man physically and therefore, to some extent, psychologically since his thrust she cannot normally stop. (It must be pointed out to the reader that the present writer is not unaware of the fact that the assumption by woman of a position in intercourse, which puts her over the man, is by no means novel. Obviously it has been practised for centuries, if not millennia, depending on the tendencies and the enjoyment requirement of one or both partners: it is a fact of life that in the sexual sphere there is nothing new under the sun, save in one respect namely the psychological one. It is here suggested that the choice, if made by woman, of this particular position in intercourse is nowadays dictated more by the thought of domination than by a more interesting search of orgasm or greater satisfaction either for herself or for her male partner.)

The present position is quite different from that prevailing in the 50s and 60s and aptly recorded by Margaret Meade[15] – echoing Freud – to the effect that vaginal orgasm was a mark of maturity because it represented the natural result of intercourse, but this was not to last and the swinging 60s gradually saw the beginning of the erosion of the importance of what Freud and Meade rated so highly.

Until then it was believed that the duty of every woman was to give herself pleasure in marriage and to enjoy sex in the same way as men did mainly, if not exclusively, through the act of copulation. The theory was that mature women would only

---

[15] *Male and Female, 1950 and re-printed as a Pelican issue in 1962*

enjoy vaginal orgasm; there was not yet any common talk of clitoral satisfaction, any clear appreciation that the clitoris had a role to perform in 'ordinary' intercourse, nor any reference to Freudian implications, despite the fact that for centuries sexologists had understood the meaning and uses of the clitoris.

Sexual freedom resulted in an enormous psychological need to redraw the picture of intercourse and, as already mentioned above, it was left to W H Masters and V E Johnson[16] to establish a central role for the clitoris. Cynically, one could say that the glorification of the clitoris resulted in the disposability of the male of the species. In passing, it is perhaps worth mentioning that there was nothing new in what William Masters and Virginia Johnson did. They were the last of a long line of scientists, anatomists, doctors, surgeons, psychologists, writers and midwives who dedicated attention to the nature and functions of the clitoris, which started with our most ancient civilisations. More detailed discussion about it can be said to have started at least as early as the 2nd century. Somewhat later, the Italian scientist Gabriele Falloppio (he of the fallopian tubes and the inventor of the condom) had an argument at the beginning of the 16th century with his compatriot Matteo Realdo Colombo

[16] *Human Sexual Response, New York, 1966*

(better known to the English as Renaldus Columbus), the latter too claiming to have discovered the clitoris.

Both claims are not accurate but there is no doubt that Colombo appreciated the clitoris better than most. He is on record as saying that it was 'pre-eminently the seat of woman's delight' and for that reason he argued that it should be called 'the love or sweetness of Venus'.

He was convinced that it should be treated as the female equivalent of the penis.

However, one of the consequences that was not fully appreciated of what Masters and Johnson did is that, coupled with the availability of the contraceptive pill, it reduced the significance of romance and courtship to the advantage of immediate sexual gratification.

Another effect of the changed perspective on relations is the increasing use of technical aids, which can be turned on and off at will. It also explains the frequency by Western women of oral intercourse. The woman is in charge of oral sexual activity, she can decide whether to see the act through to its logical conclusion.

All this results in a certain inelegance by modern woman but, above all, insensitivity on her part.

What gives woman the understanding and judgement, which she claims to possess, and is usually right in such a claim, is the emotional stability resulting from a loving relationship with a man. Deprived of that, woman is confused and selfish since her basic instincts are frustrated and thus she misses the joys and satisfaction that such a tie ought to provide for her.

These frustrated women have no brightness in their eyes, no joy in their half-baked smiles, no lilt in their step. They are cold, calculating, dull and almost unfailingly unsmiling. Sorry, girls, but that is my opinion.

CHAPTER ELEVEN – The Search for Power

In 50 years' time those who look back on our sexual relationships will be surprised to find that they seem to have gone awry at the very time when women's progressive emancipation at home and in the workplace should, in fact, have made them easier. There is a case for arguing that by creating a climate of sexual 'laissez-faire' the contraceptive pill may have dulled man's hunting instinct since woman became a much more willing prey in one sense and, in a totally different one, herself the hunter.

(One is not here advocating a life of restraint and certainly not the kind of continence, which Aldous Huxley (Antica, 1923) termed "that melancholy sexual perversion".)

Furthermore, at the moment when female emancipation should have ensured equality of rights and treatment and thus greater respect for her as an individual, sexual violence upon women – and indeed, on children of all ages – has increased at a rate never before witnessed in our history; the crime of rape, for example, becoming almost a routine occurrence. Whether these developments are due to the fact that the focus on sex, fostered by the profit motive of the media and the publishing industry principally for the purposes of entertainment and indulgence, has reached staggering proportions with the equivalent of soft-porn material vigorously promoted even in 'classy' women's periodicals, and has gone too far, is a moot point. The fact remains, however, that these unfortunate developments cannot be disputed, and are the result of an ever-increasing shift in the balance of control between men and women.

The search for power underwritten by feminists of the 18th, 19th and 20th centuries found its natural outlet, thanks to man, in the contraceptive pill. At that stage woman became in charge of her destiny since she ensured that she would only procreate when she wished and not when man decided.

Whilst initially this was a boon for unbridled manifestations of sexual activity, over the intervening decades it highlighted the ever-increasing concern of woman to assert her dominance over man, as already mentioned above.

It is hardly surprising that all the writers (psychologists, sociologists, religious observers, agony aunts) remark on the noticeable increase in oral sexual activity with a suggested resultant greater incidence of gingivitis. Woman has the choice of performing fellatio with or without a condom: she is in charge. She may decide to take the risk (slight?) of contracting HIV by unprotected oral activity, or she may not; in all probability she is not aware of the sevenfold increase over the past ten years of cancer-generating infection by HPV, the human papilloma virus. Man has little say in the matter; indeed, he may even be the loser for it would appear that communication of HPV is more common from female to male rather than otherwise.

A further consideration that supports the present approach is that the intention of modern woman to be in charge of the sexual relation and to display power over man is becoming a well-established factor in modern human affairs. It is correct to say that the more emancipated woman is, the more self-reliant on her ability to support herself without assistance from man, the more 'feminist' her tendencies, the greater her concern about self-assertiveness. The increased frequency, almost the established normality of fellatio, is in direct proportion to woman's emancipation.

Quite rightly, modern woman no longer wishes to be a slave, and there is no way that the situation will change. Lawyers have a saying that once freedom has been conferred, it can no longer be revoked.

It is noteworthy that the assertion of power by woman has found its logical outcome in the Divorce Reform Act 1969, which, as already observed, made divorce available on demand in practical terms. Statistics show that the majority of divorce petitions are lodged by women. They also show that woman is more likely to take the initiative in leaving her husband.

(More about divorce in the next chapter.)

CHAPTER TWELVE – Feminism (whatever that may mean)

The reader may perhaps be surprised that a separate chapter is being dedicated to feminism, whatever that expression means, since at first blush the concern of modern woman for equality of rights in society, in employment and in the possibility of having a career equal to that of her male counterpart, should not of itself affect her sexual performance; indeed, it ought to improve it to the benefit of her enjoyment and that of her male partner.

Whatever the theory, there is no doubt that the ever increasing assertion of her personality by woman in society and in the workplace and, above all, in family relations does affect her attitude and indeed her performance in the sexual sphere.

It is not merely a question of an ardent feminist not wishing to be man's slave. Nor is it a matter of modern western woman not wishing to be a second grade sexual performer; but she is facing increasing competition from the East.

Apart from 'technical' reasons, which are here ignored to avoid pruriency, one of the features of oriental women generally (Chinese, Japanese, Thai, Vietnamese and so on) that strikes the Western male and attracts him increasingly to them is their so-called submissiveness, at least at the sexual level. That trait seems to be disappearing as far as Western woman generally, and especially Anglo-American women, are concerned (how long such Eastern submissiveness will last, given the impact of the contraceptive pill and of Coca Cola, remains to be seen).

Whether this is a good or a bad thing for heterosexual relations is a matter about which there will remain for some time considerable debate but there is no doubt, at least in this writer's view, that an ardent feminist is less likely to be a successful heterosexual partner: ask any experienced philanderer.

There is also the consideration that if Freud is correct when he asserts that the young woman passes from a clitoral phase to a vaginal one that allows her to become a real woman, then the feminists who shun intercourse with a male and rely merely on their clitoris have, by Freud's assertion, never really grown up. If this is true it may explain why, when the feminist writers to which reference has already been made reach the age of 'maturity', they change the views they had proffered so vigorously and so inelegantly when perhaps they were less reliant on any contribution, sexual or psychological, by a poor male.

No attention will be dedicated in this essay to a damaging consequence of the application of strict feminist principles, namely some of its social, political and practical effects. As an example, the insistence on quotas in politics, teaching, public company management and so on is not always conducive to the selection of the best people for the job and it creates an echelon of privileged human beings chosen not because of their abilities but because of their sex.

One can't help observing how absurd the situation is. We have abolished the hereditary principle of selection for the House of Lords but are retaining, indeed fostering, the establishment of preferential choices based on what is alleged to be a different type of 'nobility'; but probably, considerations of this nature are not that strictly relevant to sexual behaviour. Nevertheless, the consequences (on the sexual behaviour of English women) of what has been termed generically 'feminism' cannot be ignored and a little attention will be dedicated to them.

Obviously, some caution is needed when using the term feminism since it conveys different meanings to different people and, indeed, has varying connotations depending upon the context. No attempt is made here to define it because any definition automatically amounts to a restriction and that in itself would not be acceptable to a true feminist.

One can't help observing also, however, that feminists themselves are a little uncertain about what they are supposed to be. For example, it is a little trite to say, as Dale Spender does, that "a feminist is a woman who does not accept man's socially sanctioned view of himself"[17]; a statement that seems unhelpful since there are very many women indeed who do not sing men's praises, either discordantly or in unison, but nevertheless do not go and burn their bras.

However, for present purposes some attempt must be made to define feminism and the best description is suggested to be that it is a view of nature and of life which argues that men and women are exactly the same, not only by reference to their equality before the law, but also in the physical sense (the physical equivalence of man and woman is a much less modern concept than some feminists believe. Over at least two centuries it has been argued more than once that it exists and examples are given: the vagina – or the clitoris – are the female equivalent of the penis, the ovaries are the testicles, etc; there are other similarities which are more appropriate to a medical text book).

---

[17] *Women Have Ideas, Pandora, 1982, op cit page 8*

From this the belief follows that not only are women entitled to equal rights or job opportunities (a perfectly legitimate aim) but also their physical and psychological traits, tendencies and peculiarities are to be equated to men's.

Having gone that far some feminists also argue that women are, in fact, better than men. It is hardly a coincidence that Lady Mary Wortley Montague, in her work "Woman Not Inferior to Man", claimed that the female sex was the better on the basis that *'...no one will deny but that at least upon the most modest computation, there are a thousand bad men to one bad woman'*. That does seem going over the top and has become increasingly difficult to justify nowadays, given the wider participation of young girls and women in violence and crime.

The philosopher, Bertrand Russell, put the matter in its proper perspective when in his work "Marriage and Morals"[18] he wrote: *'the rights of women did not, of course, depend upon any belief that women were morally or in other ways superior to men; they depended solely on their rights as human beings or rather upon the general argument in favour of democracy. But as always happens when an oppressed class or nation is claiming its rights, advocates sought to strengthen the general argument by their*

---

[18] *Unwin Paperbacks, London, 1976, page 59*

contention that woman had peculiar merits and these merits were generally represented as belonging to the moral order'.

The British representatives of the female sex who acted as social reformers in the 19th century certainly would not fall within Russell's classification. When Josephine Butler campaigned for well over a decade to repeal the 1846 Contagious Diseases Act and attendant legislation she was not so much concerned about whether she was better than a man but merely with protecting women, because she thought that the promiscuity existing at the time resulted in women being infected by venereal diseases, which, as she put it, was 'almost universal' amongst males.

(The spread of venereal disease being solely the fault of the male of the species was picked up again in 1913 by Christabel Pankhurst. She was the originator of the Women's Social and Political Union; she thought that about 80% of men at the time were so infected and her motto was that women should get the vote and men should be chaste).

Those who fought for the liberalisation of the laws dealing with property, which resulted in the Married Women Property Acts 1870, 1875 and 1882 certainly were not concerned about any kind of physical, psychological or moral superiority but merely with ensuring that men should not have the advantage over women when it came to property matters so that the two sexes ought to be treated equally, which obviously is just. Feminism, even assuming it existed at the time, did not come into it.

When Octavia Hill embarked on her social campaign to reform and improve the living conditions of London's poor she certainly wasn't thinking of intercourse but merely of amelioration in the state and health of the people who lived in unsanitary conditions.

When Dr Mary Scharlieb carried out her profession with dignity and morality it is probable that nothing was further from her mind than any kind of glorification of female masturbation such as has occurred in recent times.

No comparison can be made between women of this ilk and present-day feminists whose sole concern appears to be sexual rather more than social.

It is for this reason that some attention is dedicated to the theory of feminism because the practical effect on English young girls (and indeed, on British society as a whole) is detrimental.

It is detrimental because it runs counter to the physical conformation and the psychological heritage of woman.

It is not merely a matter of physical differences, which in any event cannot that easily be discounted and of which one can dispose quite easily by the observation that it certainly was not man's fault that he was created in a certain manner. More important however is the different approach to life which feminism almost by definition engenders.

The premise of feminists' thoughts seems to be that women have had enough of being slaves to men: quite rightly so. But no account is taken that one cannot divorce oneself from the factual situation of the different physical and psychological conformations nor can one overcome them merely by claiming that not all of them are acceptable to woman.

The ambition to be the equal of man creates certain inelegances of behaviour, which, if adopted by a young, susceptible, immature girl, are on the whole unpleasant.

On the 'formal' side, one can think of drunkenness, smoking, drug-taking, promiscuity, and sexual carelessness, the consequences of which we can see in our daily lives; more importantly, the loss of modesty and gentility, the flaunting of one's physical attributes and so on. If one wished to treat the matter exhaustively the litany would no doubt become boring and there is no wish here to moralise but merely to draw attention to some of the more obvious and visible manifestations of the jettisoning of the shackles of the alleged slavery of woman to man.

There have been times in English history (typical is the subjection of the woman's property to the control of the husband) when woman was in fact a slave of man, but whether we like it or not the same certainly can't be said for the 20th century and even more so for the 21st.

One of the major criticisms that can be levelled at some of our more extreme feminist writers is that, in their desire to make women more like men, they have caused them to lose their femininity by increasing their aggressiveness and thus becoming inelegant; comment has already been passed on one of the more obvious and common signs of this, namely the use of vulgar words and expressions and inelegant posture.

The counter to that is that a clear distinction should be made between sex, which is the result of biology, and gender, which is a consequence of life in society. That may be but feminists are loath to analyse any criticism levelled at such a view.

More significant even than the visible conduct are the psychological implications.

As observed above, modern women are much more anxious than their grandmothers. Whilst sex is no longer a taboo subject there seems still to be an element of perhaps guilt, certainly shame as far as English women are concerned. This arises mainly from the fact that with the disappearance of courtship any sexual heterosexual act seems inspired rather than by love, by technique. There is a constant concern about living up to certain standards, which are not generally speaking available to the majority of human beings. To assuage such concern, we have had the increasing popularity and massive sales of drugs, tranquilisers and sexual aids.

With particular reference to sexual aids, there is a consideration to be put forward applicable in particular to those feminists who shun intercourse with the male of the species. It is this author's belief that the orgasmic satisfaction obtained by a woman using sexual aids has an element of incompleteness. She usually experiences an uncontrollable feeling that something is missing;

the resultant orgasms are more often than not less satisfying than those that – man permitting... – could and should be obtained through heterosexual intercourse.

What is provoked is a sort of dissociation between the mechanical response and the absence of the psychological component that would result in a more comprehensive reaction of the kind consolidated over millennia.

It remains a fact that a machine is not really a substitute for a strong, capable man.

Further evidence of the unsatisfactory nature of sexual relations in Britain can be derived from the high rate of divorce.

In the United Kingdom there were a total of 144,071 divorce petitions in 2009 (of these 119,589 alone related to England and Wales. The total divorces for the United Kingdom in 2011 were 132,233). Of these 96,749 resulted in decrees granted to the wife and 47,205 in decrees granted to the husband. Of the grounds alleged 23,555 were for adultery whereas 62,238 were for unreasonable behaviour.

51% of the marriages (fewer and fewer) celebrated in the UK end up in divorce in less than five years. The UK has the fourth highest rate of divorce in the world (following Russia, the USA and 'Czechoslovakia').

One is, of course, entitled to ask what the connection is between the high rate of divorce and unsatisfactory sex because that is not immediately apparent. There are many reasons other than sexual relations why marriages fail.

Until the Divorce Reform Act 1969 the 'classical' grounds for divorce were adultery, cruelty, desertion, unsoundness of mind, sodomy, bestiality and rape.

There was a public official, the Queen's Proctor, who had the right to intervene where the evidence of such conduct was unsatisfactory or there had been behaviour by the parties such as connivance, condonation or collusion, which disentitled them to a divorce.

The '69 Act however revolutionised English law so that it became very simple to obtain a divorce if one of the spouses could prove the irretrievable breakdown of the marriage. The causes of such irretrievable breakdown were not only the previously codified ones but also all others that could be included in the all-embracing formulation of 'unreasonable behaviour'. Put differently, the objective test of a failed marriage was transformed into a subjective decision taken by either spouse without any real say on the part of the court. It is not difficult to see the consequences of such a shift, namely divorce at will. The 1969 Act sounded the death knell for marriages as traditionally established and understood.

(So what? New families are being created, new relationships are forged, two homes come into being instead of the single marital home; the children may even enjoy spending time in two different homes meeting other children as members of another family; often difficult to determine which family but the world is changing and the changes cannot be resisted. Such an argument too is often put forward with conviction but this author fears that the reality of these situations where the original family has broken down is unfortunately quite a sad one. A personal view, no doubt, as many others expressed in this work; but may be a correct one.)

It has not all been plain sailing after 1969. At regular intervals there are pronouncements of one kind or the other even from governments, as well as from judges, to the effect that divorce has been made too easy and for the sake of the children the law should be tightened. What is lacking however is any suggestion or indeed unanimity on how to remedy the consequences of the 1969 legislation. An interesting development in this connection occurred in September 1994 when the Principal of St Anne's College, Oxford, Ruth Deech (now Baroness Deech), recorded her opinion that "existing divorce law should be strengthened" and "an education for marriage" should be drawn up for schools. The observations are interesting because Ruth Deech was a member of the Law Commission which formulated the Divorce Reform Act 1969 and was honest enough to acknowledge that she made a mistake in voting for that Act.

She was, of course, right. Little did our legislators realise that they were sowing the seed for the destruction of the cohesion of British society.

The results would be inevitable: disrespect for any kind of moral code, sexual or otherwise, and the paving of the road to violence, social unrest and anarchy.

The collapse of the family, the building block of society and of the State, would cause the disappearance in our youngsters of any sense of belonging, of discipline in our schools and the increasing appearance of lawlessness on the streets.

Still, one is entitled to ask what the connection is and the answer it is here suggested is to be found in the statistics indicated above.

Adultery (whether on its own or as part of the all-embracing formula of 'unreasonable behaviour'), is the first cause for divorce. It is established that when a husband sues for divorce he alleges adultery by his wife in at least half of the cases. This does not mean that adultery was the only ground for divorce because, even in those cases where the facts of separation or desertion have been proved by the husband on the part of his wife, it is probable that there was adultery by her as well. Indeed, in today's world it is most unlikely that where the wife is living apart from the husband or is separated from him by consent, she has not herself committed adultery: the modern ethos and the independence of woman dictate that this should be so and, in any event, in situations of marital conflict woman asserts her independence from her husband principally by sleeping with another man, an understandable psychological reaction in a tit-for-tat situation.

(In fact, the more feministic the beliefs of a woman who is offended by her husband's adultery, the more likely it is that she in turn will wish to forget about her marital vows: 'I'll show him'.)

Statistics establish this quite clearly, but the conclusion is not drawn, namely that in all such situations the wife cannot possibly have been satisfied with the husband's behaviour generally but more specifically with his sexual performance (one is ignoring for present purposes what could be termed 'casual' adultery). Statistics show that more men sue for divorce on the grounds of their wives' adultery than women in respect of their husbands' infidelity. Figures also show that this is the situation in about 40% of divorce cases, namely that the wife was not satisfied with the husband's sexual performance[19].

One can counter that, at the end of the day, there is no difference between adultery by a husband and adultery by a wife but this is not a view that is shared here, at least in the sense that one must acknowledge the different attitudes of men and women to adultery. There is a difference between the two types of adultery and it is the result of woman's child-bearing function. There is a lot to be said for the theory that, on the whole, a

[19] *Marriage and Divorce Statistics, HMSO, Series FM*

woman who is happy and sexually satisfied in a relationship with her male partner (whether married to him or not) does not develop any wish to interfere with that relationship on a sexual plane or, indeed, at all and in all likelihood – but who knows for certain what goes on in the minds of women, especially modern young women... – is probably not tempted to look at another man in sexual terms. The reason put forward by some writers for this theory is that woman has an inherent sexual stability which man lacks and which is directly attributable to her procreation function. Given the 'progress' made by women in sexual activity generally, especially since the introduction of the contraceptive pill, this seems to have become an argument which is increasingly difficult to support.

It is often argued that in so far as some men commit adultery they are merely being prompted by their natural instinct whereas women are, in all likelihood, guided by their man's neglect, inability or even impotence. This argument is, in the main, put forward by men and is of course an extremely convenient one and as such has been, with justification, considerably criticised. On the other hand, any suggestion that the above consideration is the result of male chauvinism can be easily countered by the scientific observation that man, albeit in modern days in ever-reducing quantity, produces millions of sperm cells, whereas for the purposes of fertilisation women only produce one egg. The male of the species may certainly be more 'generous'; woman is much more valuable.

But there is a more fundamental distinction to be made, at least in this writer's view. Woman's sexual passions and leanings originate in her brain; man's excitability is physical, not mental. Heterosexual males may be able to verify the truth of this statement checking their reactions when they admire a fine pair of legs or any other striking part of a woman's body.

But the likelihood is that the principal negative effect of feminism has resulted in a very noticeable lack of restraint by modern women of all ages, but especially young ones.

The feminist argument has already been set out above; but it ignores a fundamental physical difference and the fascinating, if not complicated, reproductive system of the female. It is clear that God, nature, the Big Bang or anything else one would prefer as a primary cause in the existence of the world and of human beings intended that the essential function of woman was the reproductive one. As an adjunct, she might also derive some enjoyment from the act of intercourse aimed primarily at reproduction. But in the view of the present writer this was almost an ancillary development, an added benefit, if one could put it that way, of perpetuating the species or, as psychologists would say, a pleasurable incentive to achieving that result.

(For present purposes, one is ignoring the fact that some women genetically cannot conceive.)

Feminists however take a different view. Woman's essential organic features are primarily aimed at the same enjoyment, which man derives from his own reproductive system, which in itself is self-defeating without the assistance of a woman. (The one-sex theory, which equates the reproductive organs of the male and female though reversed, has been canvassed through the ages.)

The moment this decision was taken, it was inevitable that in the same way as men are alleged to lack self-control and self-discipline in sexual matters, woman should be the same. The result is that whereas we all know that men are pigs, women nowadays lack self-restraint.

It is here suggested that lack of restraint is an all-embracing expression, which includes amongst its most important features lack of self respect or respect for one's body.

Such lack of respect is also evidenced by the decision to sacrifice, if that be the right term to use, one's virginity at a very early age indeed.

The point has already been made above that a decision of this nature taken at an early age may be dictated by a lack of understanding as to the significance of the essential features of sexual integrity; feminists however have taken the matter very much further and have approached it in two ways: either by maintaining that virginity should be preserved and not surrendered to the male at all or that it has no meaning whatsoever and can therefore be lost, in one form or the other, at any time.

But the loss of virginity at an early age and presumably before marriage – indeed almost so by definition – has possibly a further consequence, namely that when it gets to marriage there is nothing in the physical sense that the bride can offer to her spouse.

It may, of course, be a coincidence – indeed, given the changed social circumstances, it probably is – that we can no longer argue, as was done in the past, that a wife who was a virgin on getting married was less likely to divorce than one who wasn't.

This rather 'old' view has been strongly challenged by modern sociologists and psychologists. Nevertheless, one should record that Freud himself makes the related point (see "On Sexuality: Three Theories on The Theory of Sexuality". The Pelican Freud Library, Volume 7, especially page 280) that the taboo surrounding virginity is such that woman's immature sexuality discharges onto the man who first makes her acquainted with the sexual act and thus establishes the state of bondage of her to him which, with the passage of time, develops into a form of hostile bitterness, which never completely disappears throughout the marriage but nevertheless is a factor that may contribute to strengthening the relation between the parties. Admittedly, the above view – that a woman who was a virgin at marriage is less likely to divorce than one who wasn't – is rather quaint and old-fashioned; but one can't keep wondering whether, indeed, the increased rate of divorce in the UK is due to the fact that women get married having already tasted man, as the expression goes...

---------------- oOo -------------------

The intention and ambition of feminists, old and new, for official recognition of equal treatment of woman with man is coincident with woman's insistence to be allowed to perform all the jobs normally done by her male counterpart. This attitude is part and parcel of the otherwise wholly laudable striving for a full, legally acknowledged recognition of equality, which is, in itself, irreproachable and in any event, inevitable as a matter of principle whatever may be the difficulties of its execution in detail and in practice.

Unfortunately, there are a few side effects to the new feminists' order (as we have already observed) and of these the most awkward and aesthetically repugnant is woman's increased vulgarity whether she be English, French, Italian doesn't seem to matter. In modern times woman's speech has become interspersed with words and expletives, imported in the main from the USA, which are objectively unbecoming, if not demeaning. It is interesting that at the same time, and almost as an inevitable concomitant, woman manifests her dissent when she is referred to as a lady rather than as a woman, as though by choosing for her a more dignified form of address man was distracting from the validity of her newly acquired position as his equal.

Similarly, a number of people have observed that the pitch of her voice has become more shrill and is coupled with a tendency to raise its level beyond any reasonable and acceptable degree of intensity, even where it doesn't amount to shouting when speaking; almost a form of protest which follows from a psychological imbalance of one kind or the other.

Woman's delicacy has gone at the same time as her assertiveness and aggressiveness have increased; whether this is the reason why many men now shun the opposite sex and prefer either the company of other males, or of prostitutes whose vulgarity is, in manner of speaking, constitutional, must be a matter for debate. Apologies for being somewhat repetitive...

It may, of course, be entirely a coincidence but Freud had correctly anticipated the aggressiveness that emancipated woman would display. His justification for such aggressiveness was the desire of woman to rectify the imbalance caused by what he termed 'penis envy'. However, nowadays this does not seem entirely appropriate as a psychological justification. Modern women are right when they say that they do not envy men their bodies. The problem that any exasperated feminist has to face is not the absence of a penis but the more fundamental difficulty of the complex physical conformation of woman, which is a function of her pre-ordained theoretical role of child-bearing. But let us leave these psychological considerations apart.

Equally, it is hardly surprising to be told by our psychologists that women's thoughts are, generally speaking, becoming increasingly obscene. Obscenity is, in great part, lack of style and extremist modern English woman certainly lacks that. Her clothes and her perfume may come from Balenciaga but they are not sufficient to cover up either these inelegances or the smell engendered by vulgarity of manner and, above all, of thought.

It may be somewhat easy at this stage to accuse this author of chauvinism and misogyny. The counter to that may well be to suggest to the reader that he/she looks around with ears and eyes open...

Also to be imputed to feminists is the belief that modern woman is capable of encompassing both lewd and loving emotions, thus providing a total outlet for man's sexual desires, of whichever type they may be; this is a form of naive, wishful thinking. The Americans have, in fact, gone so far as to suggest that high-heels produce happy homes. Whether this means that a wife should also be a tart is a little difficult to determine from this side of the Atlantic; and in any event, has not proved a good recipe for successful matrimony given the high rate of divorce in the USA (does the reader need reminding that the said country has, after Russia, the second highest rate of divorce in the world?

Interesting that the two still most powerful nations in the world have the highest rate of divorce. Is there a moral to be drawn from this? The answer is left to my few readers).

The difficulty inherent in the belief in the all-embracing capacity of woman, which appears to be spreading in England, is that it is far too convenient to argue that the woman of the 21st century can, if she believes it, in fact be wife, partner, mistress, mother, sister, breadwinner and friend at the same time. She can procreate, fornicate, appreciate, listen sympathetically to, and cater for all the passions, the failings and, at times, the deviations of her man; and still earn a living.

The trouble is that such an outstandingly capable, compassionate and understanding human being has yet to be born. It is conceivable, of course, that the next millennium may see something of the kind come into existence as a result of genetic engineering but there is, at present, an element of 'hubris' in feminist dogma since no woman exists who has the physical and, above all, the emotional and psychological strength and ability to be all things to her husband (or as one says nowadays, partner), let alone looking after her children, if any.

This is not solely an English problem since a similar difficulty is to be found in most countries in the Western world. The man who has known more than one woman can't possibly agree with such feminist tenet. He would probably state unhesitatingly that a creature of this ilk, such a paragon of all virtues feminine, Amazon of the marital and non-bed chamber, indefatigable and undaunted, athlete of womanhood, never tired, off-colour, irritable or irritating, always conscious of the need to please her mate at any time of the day and night and at whatever cost to herself, is a pure figment of the imagination of most feminists (and writers of cheap novels).

Another way in which the obsession with matters sexual finds an almost indecent manifestation is what one could term the confessional tendency, which the so-called ladette culture has engendered.

People in the public eye, and not too rarely even public figures of some importance, seem to relish providing details of their private lives and in giving descriptions of their sexual performances whether on a table in the basement of a well-known central London restaurant after closing time or by having sexual relations in very close proximity to the bells of Big Ben.

Until recent times it was unheard of that matters such as these should be made known by public figures. It is often maintained that such "reluctance" to condescend to particulars of sexual activity was the result of a puritan upbringing. That may not however be the full story since it can be argued that, certainly as far as woman is concerned, revelations of this nature would in the normal course of life have been precluded by a sense of modesty, which is directly related to her procreative function. It is hardly a coincidence that one often hears the remark being made that English young girls of the 20th and 21st centuries quite clearly lack modesty in their behaviour, attire and, increasingly, have a tendency to adopt rather vulgar postures – which are invariably inelegant – or indulge in offensive conduct.

These attitudes are encouraged by the free availability of pornographic images (some people might say that this is too polite a word for them, the adjective 'disgusting' springing to mind) on a number of internet sites whose providers do not appear to be unduly concerned that, for example, girls under age might wish to display themselves in explicit images available to the general public without any form of aesthetic constraint. Pornography, especially that freely available to young children and children of all ages, seems to be our English plague of the decade.

When statements like this are made, as they are from time to time in the press and on television, voices are often heard to the effect that this is simply a phase. Our children will not be bothered for too long about pornographic representations; they will learn to distinguish between one and the other and decide which theme is to be believed and accepted. This is a most fallacious argument because it presupposes in our children an ability to discriminate in a field, that of human sexuality, which has defeated grown-up men and women of all ages and nationalities over the centuries.

The concern that the flaunting of pointed sexual images before young children is dangerous, which we do not nowadays appear to take too much to heart, goes back a very long time.
The Latin poet Sextus Propertius published in the year 29BC one of the works for which he is still very well known, namely his 'Elegies'.

In one of them (2.6.27) he rails against the practice in some rich households, of having erotic depictions on walls of the kind that are still to be seen amongst the ruins of Pompei. This appears to have been for him a recent practice since he states in terms that in earlier times homes were not decorated with objectionable representations of nakedness and sexual activity.

He objects in turn to the corruption of the minds, especially of young girls, and goes so far as to suggest that those guilty of such conduct should be blinded... as punishment.

Again, one can't help reaching the conclusion, which may come as some surprise to present-day pornographers, that there is nothing really new under the sun.

On a slightly different topic, and most regrettably, there are very cogent arguments to support the claim that the so-called egalitarian principles that are said to inspire feminist thought have inevitably resulted in the establishment of the concept of political correctness (a suggestion I have already made but definitely worth repeating). That is unfortunate, since the absurdities engendered in everyday life and in English society by a strict adherence to concepts, which are said to be politically correct but which are most practically inconvenient, are too well known to require elaboration.

CHAPTER THIRTEEN – What's The Point of Virginity Anyhow?

A major difficulty that confronts any student of modern attitudes to virginity appears to be the reluctance to consider what it means since there are no official studies, little reliable data and no certainty whatsoever about any of the quaint theories concerning it that are propounded at regular intervals nowadays in the press and on the television screens of Western countries.

It is often said that it is only people from the Mediterranean countries and the Arabs who, at least until recently, had a penchant for virginity.

This is not strictly accurate. A valuation of virginity in women has been around for a very long time, as any student of Greek and Roman societies will no doubt know. It would be outside the scope of this small work to consider it in an historical context going back centuries but it may be interesting to compare the attitude of the Victorians with the present-day approach.

The desire for young virgins was facilitated by the spread of child prostitution in England, especially in the 18th and 19th centuries. The obsession of the upper classes and of the aristocracy with virginity found a natural outlet in the poverty of most social strata and it was the indigent parents themselves who, in order to survive, offered their daughters as sacrificial lambs. The girls were forced to surrender themselves at ages as early as 12 and 13. But this is hardly surprising because in those days young children starting at eight were sent out to work with a life expectancy of less than ten years; a practice particularly evident in northern England where the textile trade was such an important feature, highly damaging health-wise for young people.

The indiscriminate search for virgins to some extent depreciated the value of the commodity and it is probably true to say that, in most cases, something of great value, the most prized possession at that time (and maybe even today!) of any young woman, was sacrificed to men who hardly had the ability to appreciate what they were taking, either because of natural insensitivity or drunkenness. Quite high on the list of such abusers of young girls were, especially in the 18th and 19th centuries, the members and frequenters of the so-called “gentlemens’ clubs” in the St James’s area of London.

Throughout recorded history virginity has always been prized even at the cost of cheating the poor male by the long-established and sometimes traditional device of fixing the date of the consummation of the wedding to coincide with a particular time in the menstrual cycle. Even in those circumstances where, having been lost, virginity had to be, so to say, re-instated, human resourcefulness knew no bounds. From little bags of blood that burst on impact to the use of pigeon bladders or anylin dyes, comfrey baths, leeches, sea onion, drugs to tighten vaginal muscles and, much more recently, hymenoplasty (vaginal reconstruction), carried out expensively by Harley Street surgeons, human ingenuity knew, and still knows, few bounds.

The reader might just be interested to know what vaginal reconstruction is. Hymenoplasty is the recreation of the vulva with torn tissue. The practice is that a new membrane is inserted in a gelatine-like substance, the lining of the vagina being used to recreate the hymen, the whole then being stitched back together. In the modern version of the pigeon bladder, a blood capsule is inserted into the vagina to ensure realism. Surprising what women will get up to...

The search for virginity has always been a fancy on the part of wealthy philanderers. It should not be thought for a moment that all the Victorians assumed that women were virtuous before marriage since there is evidence that the more respectable people, especially of the middle class, were quite content to indulge in pre-marital sexual activity. Nevertheless, in Victorian times, the demand for young virgins was very great indeed and the poverty of the country made it easier or at least more morally acceptable for parents actually to sell their daughters into a particular form of sexual slavery, which was fairly common. Even in more recent days, there was in London a Queenie Gerald who began life as a prostitute at a very early age and who ran a brothel near Piccadilly Circus as recently as the years before the First World War. Her specialisation was the provision of “nice, sweet, virgin morsels”. It is in connection with this trade that she and others before her developed numerous techniques for fooling the customer into believing that the girl who was offering herself to him was, in fact, a virgin for which he had to pay a substantial sum of money, since virgins commanded a much higher price than an ordinary prostitute. At that time, the price for having the opportunity of deflowering a young girl ranged from 20 to 50 Guineas, the modern approximate equivalent of such sum ranging between £500 and £1,000; a fortune, really.

Probably the most notable and publicised event relating to this particular English trade was the intervention of the editor of the Pall Mall Gazette, William Thomas Stead, who, in accord with sound principles of journalism, created his own news.

In 1885, he posed as a client, found a couple willing to sell their daughter, and "bought" one young girl, a virgin named Eliza. He then took her to one of the many "midwives" whose job it was to certify the virginity of girls, had her so certified, and then went to a room where he threatened to deflower her. Instead of doing so however he published his own story and acquired great notoriety, not always that favourable, for a very long time for himself and indeed for his Pall Mall Gazette.

He was charged with 'kidnapping' and sent to prison for three months but his intervention resulted in a boon for Josephine Butler and her companions who were up in arms against the abuse provoked by the existence of the Contagious Diseases Acts 1846 and 1864, which allowed the police to use primitive metal instruments to 'inspect' women who were prostitutes or who were denounced as being of loose habits. The furore caused by Stead's enterprise and, above all, the consequential campaign orchestrated by Josephine Butler resulted in two fundamental decisions by Parliament. The first was to raise the age of consent to 16 and the second, the year after these events, to repeal the Contagious Diseases legislation.

The name of the magazine in question, the Pall Mall Gazette, is not at all a coincidence. The whole of the area of Pall Mall, St

James's Street and Jermyn Street had, for many centuries, been known for its brothels. Such a tradition is not only a glorious but also a royal one. The masses of foreign tourists who, nowadays, walk around St James's admiring the architecture and the shops would find it difficult to believe that a great part of it was, up to almost the end of the 19th century, not only unpaved and unlit, but in the main dedicated to whoring. Prostitutes were first encouraged to this particular locality because of the existence of the Royal Palace of St James's (and indeed some of them remained in the area even after the court moved to Buckingham Palace). Apart from the 'nunneries' opposite the Palace (where young country girls were taught, sometimes very violently and clumsily, the rudiments of sexual life) and the 'bagnios' (initially Turkish-style bathing establishments that later easily became dens of sexual corruption in the same manner as the various massage parlours of central London and of other main cities have extended the scope of the 'massaging activities' despite the occasional displayed notice saying 'no sex'), many of the houses and buildings in the St James's area now occupied by respectable shopkeepers, trading companies, institutions and professional people, were brothels of a more or less high class. Nor is it a coincidence that the famous 'gentlemen's clubs' of Pall Mall and St James's were established in close proximity to the whoring grounds of the St James's area and St James's Park. It is in the particular locality that a very brisk trade in virgins took place, especially in the 17th and 18th centuries.

The reader who is interested in the subject and who may be inclined to verify what kind of activities took place in what are nowadays quite respectable buildings in Pall Mall and St James's may wish to refer to "Royal St James's" by E J Burford (Robert Hale, London, 1988) and "Wits, Wenches and Wantons" by the same author (Robert Hale, London 1986), which make very interesting reading.

There is, of course, nothing unusual about the desire for a virgin, which was developed by men throughout history. There is something almost pathological about man's desire for virginity: it is as though he relishes the thought of corrupting something fresh and white, like putting blood on snow or having the sensation of climbing Everest for the first time: nobody else had been there before him (such almost poetic considerations obviously are somewhat out of fashion and, indeed, sound rather quaint to modern ears).

In former years, one of the justifications adduced for the provision of young virgins was that they were supposed to be good for older men. This belief can be traced back to the Bible, where reference is made to King David being advised to allow a young virgin to 'warm him'. It is certainly an acknowledged feature of everyday life that as the male of the species gets older, he has a tendency to prefer younger women, whether virgins or not. But it may be carrying male selfishness and chauvinism a trifle too far to maintain, without qualification, that young virgins are 'good', whatever that expression may mean, for older men. Such younger women may well give an 'old man' a heart attack...

There also existed the odd belief (mistaken or more probably convenient) that intercourse with a virgin was a cure for the ravages of syphilis!

It is difficult to determine why modern English men, especially younger men, when tackled about whether they would wish their wife to be a virgin or not, seem to attach little or no significance to the particular feature. It is, of course, true that sexual customs change through the ages but one would have thought that such a fundamental feature of woman might still be of interest to men.

It no longer appears to have any real significance in the choice of a wife. Trying to analyse the reasons for this one can only draw the conclusion that modern English man is like the fox in Aesop's fable who was trying to eat grapes in a vineyard but could not reach the bunches because the vines were trained on trellises, which were too high for her. She went away frustrated, deciding that she did not really want the grapes after all because they were not sufficiently ripe... Put differently, it is not there; accordingly I don't want it.

Perhaps one should not be too concerned about the early loss of virginity. One is not unmindful of the fact that in his Leningrad Notebook (1735-1750) the French philosopher Voltaire wrote 'it is one of the superstitions of the human mind to have imagined that virginity could be a virtue'. But then, social conditions were different in his day; although perhaps we should take what he said with a modicum of salt.

Traditionally, it was believed that a woman who surrendered her virginity prior to marriage lacked respect for her own body. It is conceivable that there is an element of truth in that belief. If so, it can also be argued that a man is normally aware of the behaviour and reactions of a woman who lacks respect for herself and the direct consequence of that is lack of respect for her by him.

The problem is that respect doesn't grow on trees like spaghetti; it is a very delicate plant, which needs a lot of attention, consideration and almost loving care.

The lack of it is, in a sense, contagious. The man who has no respect for the woman will end up by having no respect for himself. This will result in his ignoring any sense of honour in the same way as the dishonourable Members of Parliament, who have been shown recently to have committed irregularities and, indeed, even crimes in claiming their expenses, have come to the fore in increasing numbers. Not for them, obviously, any thought of resigning.

There is thus created a vicious circle in the sense that the man who doesn't respect the woman because she doesn't respect herself ends up by not respecting himself and acting dishonourably, causing the woman in turn to have no respect for him. This seems to be a fairly common problem in modern English society and without wishing to moralise in any sense, is an aspect of our behaviour which is worthy of much closer attention than is normally dedicated to it.

Having got this far, one of the many objections that the reader may raise is that undue attention has been dedicated to the behaviour of our young girls and not enough to that of our young boys whose conduct in a sexual context – and indeed in that of violence towards women – is just as significant, more particularly because it is becoming increasingly offensive and violent.

More than once it has been observed that it does not suffice to blame our young girls for what is happening to them without apportioning that blame to the male of the species. As a result more than once it has been said that the boys should not only be taught sexual education but, above all, to behave as gentlemen.

The observation is, of course, quite pertinent because gentlemanly conduct is the last thing that we can expect at the moment from our male youth and, indeed, the last thing that forms part of the teaching in sex education classes. There is however a major difficulty about such an argument and it is that, whether we like it or not and whatever view we may adopt of sexual behaviour in our country, gentlemen do not normally exist where there are no ladies (in passing, one cannot resist the temptation of observing how odd in the third millennium is the use of the words 'gentlemen' and 'ladies'...). It is the 'lady-like' behaviour of a young girl that guides the approach and the conduct of a young boy and not the other way round. As applies even to more mature people, a woman who behaves sexually in a certain manner will almost invariably elicit a similar sexual response from a man (I am obviously ignoring the crime of rape). If a young girl behaves like a tart, as many unfortunately do nowadays, she cannot expect her male companion to behave with any kind of dignity, forbearance and appreciation. This is a variant of the 'respect' argument already proffered above, expressed rather more crudely, but no less correctly.

Whether we wish to acknowledge it or not, in the sexual relationship it is woman who dictates the pace, the standard and, to some extent, even the quality. Granted that it is perfectly true that our young boys should take a course in good manners in addition to sex instruction, the same should be said of our young girls. After all, it takes two to tango.

Cynically, one could say that honour and respect in England have gone down the drain; the drain itself is overflowing. For present purposes suffice it to say that this is probably the major indictment of any kind of feminist "philosophy", an aspect of the debate that has been picked up in an earlier chapter. Of course, one cannot impute to feminist philosophy the disgusting (sexual or otherwise) behaviour of many of our youngsters; but the aura surrounding the behaviour of young girls does, whether we like it or not, directly contribute to a lack of restraint on the part of young boys.

One of the principal problems that the earlier date of intercourse produces is the consideration that when a woman postponed her loss of virginity until marriage and when her 'policy' as regards that particular part of her anatomy was that it would only become available to a man who was prepared to be patient and by his patience to show his commitment to, and his desire for her, the giving of herself by a woman was an occurrence which had significance for her (by modern standards, a highly unusual approach), for the man and for society as a whole. That particular part of female anatomy had a value so it was thought not sensible that it should be lost casually or casually offered to all and sundry: the result was that woman felt committed by the giving of herself and so was more likely to bind her ravisher to her with the consequence that the resultant marital status was more likely to last. What happens nowadays when people marry is that there can be almost by definition no 'surrender' of the woman to her spouse, since she has already in all likelihood surrendered herself to more than one other partner/spouse and most probably also to her spouse. Thus there is no obvious commitment by her to her spouse and vice versa and for this reason, if the relationship begins to founder, it is so much easier to terminate it than to work hard to make a success of it.

This at least is the theory, which can be said to derive some slight support from a study recorded in an article in the Journal of Sex Research, December 2012 issue, by the title "Differing Relationships When Sex Happens Before, On or After First Dates" (authors Brian Willoughby, Jason Carol, Dean Busby of Bingham Young University). The authors found that when intercourse occurred on the first date the relationship did not really blossom and at a year's term was beginning to break. It is somewhat unfortunate that any longer term effects were not considered.

A further problem with early intercourse is that, as ample evidence now shows, the majority (it is stated to be at least 98%) of women who have sexual relations at an early age complain about their experience of their first sexual encounter. This is hardly surprising. Consider the following: just suppose that the young English girl of between the ages of 15 and 16 does not have intercourse with a grown man older than 24 years of age because, by definition, such intercourse would be illegal under the present laws of England; it is more than likely that her partner will be a young boy, probably of her same age group.

Theoretically at least, his ability and experience in sexual terms are suspect.

More particularly, the girl will surrender herself in all likelihood to conform to the expectations of her peers and the 'mores' of our society. Given the way our youngsters appear to behave nowadays it is not far-fetched to say that there is a good chance that she might be half or totally drunk, either on alcohol or on drugs. That cannot possibly be an exciting experience for her as the data recorded above show beyond a shadow of a doubt.

Most girls who report either to their friends or their parents, counsellor or psychotherapist on an early loss of virginity say that they derived no pleasure from it whatsoever; practically all add that it was most unfortunate experience and all of them wished that they had not done so at such an early age. Indeed, a later study (December 3rd, 2011) collated evidence that even amongst those who lost their virginity between the ages of 18 and 24 the rate of dissatisfaction with their action was one in five; but that is by-the-by.

In the case of early intercourse between two youngsters one should not ignore the fact that, whilst the pain for the girl may not be too great for a number of reasons (for example, the prior use of tampons and the possibly still undeveloped penis), the circumstance that the young boy will, in all probability, be an insensitive oaf, a fumbling creature, a selfish, weak partner, all in all a poor specimen of manhood, may leave an indelible mark on a comparatively sensitive young girl. There is no evidence, yet, to show that the result of such an unsatisfactory type of intercourse may prompt the young girl to develop lesbian tendencies. That is something which may well be deserving of further enquiry and is undoubtedly outside the scope of the present exercise but in circumstances such as those described above, heterosexuality is under pressure and, especially in our Western society, the milieu in which the girl finds herself after a bad experience of this nature is such that it is all too easy for her to develop contempt for man. That modern woman has contempt for modern man is so self-evident that no further comment is required except perhaps to say that it may well be that in England such contempt is well deserved.

If the matter is viewed in an historical context, then it can be described as an ironical state of affairs. Starting with Mary Wortley Montague and Mary Wollstonecraft in the 18th century and ending with the more aggressive feminists of the 20th, women's struggle to achieve parity with man and equal rights in society has been a hard one.

The battle has been bitterly fought and woman has shown her mettle and, although perhaps not in the absolute social sense, she has achieved legal parity with man. But what has she done all this for?

To lose her virginity at a very early age indeed, in circumstances where she derives no pleasure from the particular exercise and, above all, would appear to live to regret having indulged in it.

It has been argued that too early a loss of virginity or, if you like, indulging at too early an age in sexual intercourse is a sideline of the "moral" consumerism and incontinence of our society, which must be coupled with the disappearance of standards, whether they be religious or of a family nature.

There are, of course, a number of environmental and social reasons why this is happening.

Reference has already been made to the fact that our young girls are maturing much more quickly but we should not ignore that they are encouraged more and more to wear clothes in their youth which of themselves highlight their sexual attributes. As observed, they may more or less happily and quite inconsistently rely on the sexual education imparted to them in schools and on safe contraception. At the end of the day, however, it is here suggested that the primary cause is lack of self-control, a point already made above.

Whether this be true or not must be a matter of argument but there appears to be little doubt that the young girls who indulge in sexual intercourse at too early an age probably do so because, whatever the reason may be, they lack some form of restraint.

The resultant lack of restraint often provokes vulgarity; of thought, of words and of posture. Indeed, some modern psychologists (mainly men, of course!) have reported that present day woman's thoughts are becoming increasingly lewd, lascivious and greedy at an especially early age, as any modern philanderer will confirm.

At the other end of the scale one should note a somewhat novel, if not interesting, and fairly recent development in the behaviour of young English women is the decision not to have intercourse. Full stop. Whether not to have intercourse until marriage or not at all isn't entirely clear.

This development definitely comes to us from the USA where, in recent times, there have been a number of pronouncements by politicians as to the ‘intactness’ of women, especially younger ones, and there have come to the fore the so-called Purity Pledges, which young school girls are supposed to take, the Virgins for Christ Movement, the publicly stated policy of some States that women should be virgins until marriage because the maidenhead was a ‘gift’ left in store for the future husband, and so on.

Whilst the number of such women, of whatever nationality, is difficult to assess, comments appear from time to time in newspapers by women who have decided to retain their virginity whilst making it clear that they are not ruling out indulging in other forms of sexual activity.

A very brief analysis of this development is probably worthwhile. Before indulging in it, however, the question springs spontaneous whether any of these ‘virgins’ ever paused and considered their physical make-up.

In all likelihood it never occurred to them to enquire whether God, Mother Earth, a female God, or the Big Bang (depending, of course, on one’s beliefs) may not have had a reason for the body and the functions attributed to woman, which are clearly and almost exclusively aimed, at least in theory, at procreation. Be that as it may.

Of course, it is always open to woman to remain a virgin out of religious conviction: some nuns do. But considerations of a religious kind appear to be much less relevant in the 21st century.

More significantly, however, there are other possible reasons for the retention of virginity. Of these, are what one would term generally hygienic thoughts, a constitutional dislike of man, a consequent decision to assert power over the male of the species and, ultimately, selfishness?

It is doubtful that any decision to remain a virgin whilst at the same time leaving it open to indulge in other sexual activity, results from hygienic considerations. Whilst sexual behaviour other than intercourse still carries some risk of catching forms of venereal diseases, it is unlikely that this consideration is foremost in the mind of the so-called ‘new virgins’.

More probable is the fact that these women do not like men and therefore do not wish to submit to them in any form. Since intercourse is one of the principal ways in which a woman might consider that she is inferior to man (she is wrong, of course, but that is a separate issue) it is easy to draw the conclusion that woman should remain a virgin. Perhaps she will lose her virginity in other forms, a description of which is avoided for the sake of decency. The decision of modern woman to exercise power over man has already been dealt with above: clearly this is a most significant contributory factor.

However, it is this writer's view that modern women who decide to remain virgins 'tout court' are motivated mainly by selfishness, perhaps even snobbery in the sense that a woman of that ilk wishes to distinguish herself from others around her. It is often claimed that this is a manifestation of 'self esteem', a form of protection of the woman's self-respect and 'spiritual' satisfaction. The difficulty in accepting justifications of this kind is that, in the majority of cases, these virginal creatures are very keen to advertise their frame of mind and body.

Perhaps the most sensible explanation of an attitude which in a sense runs counter to nature and to what woman is meant to represent is that it has become fashionable to be different; perhaps a sense of insecurity has developed in these women and they feel cosseted by their integrity.

In the case of a woman who decides to retain her virginity until she meets Mr Right, perhaps a praiseworthy decision of course, one must ask what happens in case she doesn't have such a fortunate encounter. That is a more difficult topic but one thing is certain in the present writer's view, namely that a woman's decision to remain a virgin for the rest of her life will take some time to become popular as a general policy.

But enough about virginity. Nowadays, there really doesn't seem to be much point to it in any case.

CHAPTER FOURTEEN – Our History is Our Sexual Destiny

It may well be true, as atheists, secularists and others of different opinion or belief have been maintaining for some years with increasingly raucous voices, that England is no longer a Christian country (there are also some who now maintain that it never was).

From this follows the prescription that there should be no public evidence of Christianity, no too obvious crosses as necklaces (unless the European Court of Human Rights decides to extend considerably its recent – January 2013 – judgement in the BA employee case), none on crematoria buildings, no more traditional prayers at Council meetings and the ever-increasing related denials of any significant display of Christian religious beliefs to enforce quaint concepts of political correctness and avoid "upsetting" those who do not believe in the Resurrection (will it be long before claims are made that we should change the words of our national anthem? After all, there seems no point in praying for the health of the monarch to God, if He does not exist...).

It remains an arguable point whether views of this kind are right; but of one thing we can be absolutely certain, namely that such was not the position in England before the 1960s (the reasons why this decade proved so significant for our country are dealt with in Chapter Six).

Certainly England's Christianity dates backs to the days of St Augustine and continued uninterrupted.

From the 16th century until the arrival of the contraceptive pill, open declarations of male and female homosexuality and of feminism, England was a country of strong Christian beliefs often enforced with brutality where adultery, fornication and other sexual deviations were concerned.

It was because of England's Christianity that Henry VIII had problems with the Pope, which, unresolved, kick-started the Reformation.

What better evidence of the fact that England was a Christian country than the beautiful and architecturally typical cathedrals scattered around England? One wonders how those who deny Christianity can account for so many and so outstanding examples of perseverance and faith.

However, the nature of that belief had often rather typical manifestations.

It was an unforgiving type of Christian creed with its persecution of sexual irregularity; it was as though throughout the periods of the Reformation, Victorian and Edwardian England the principle of forgiveness, which is a tenet of Christian belief, had been thrown out of the window.

An example of this attitude is the way in which English society through the said periods reacted to prostitutes. Views alternated between consideration of the prostitutes as children of the devil, on the one hand and, at differing periods, the manifestation by society on the other hand of extremes of pity for these poor creatures who were victims of rakes, bawds and ultimately violent lustful males. A balance was seldom struck between the two views.

(As an aside, it could be said that the balance hasn't yet been reached, given our ambiguous attitude to the suggested decriminalisation of prostitution activity; but that is another story.)

Indeed, so interested in matters sexual were our ancestors of the Elizabethan and Jacobean period that performances of plays dealing with prostitutes and brothel keepers were very common. Especially those prostitutes who were a cut above the average, if one were to use that expression, became very well known and were the subject of talk, gossip, news and sometimes admiration and envy in the same way as modern actresses and footballers.

This approach continued well into the 18th century as some of Hogarth's prints confirm.

Such notoriety was mainly fostered by the major increase in circulation, particularly in the cities, of newspapers, pamphlets and books. Printing in England received a boost at this time particularly towards the end of the 17th and the remainder of the 18th centuries.

It would take too long to analyse in detail another factor contributory to what is here described as the impacted sexual psyche of the English people - that is, its Calvinist/Protestant traditions (which have always clashed with the Catholic approach to matters sexual).

This different attitude we certainly owe to our German cousins with whom we share many of the sexual characteristics which are mentioned in this work. It may not come amiss to observe that Protestantism was born in northern climes whereas Catholicism was born, so to say, in the Mediterranean. The extent to which meteorological factors influence religion is not something which falls within the purview of observations on sexual behaviour; but the differences between the two religious currents are certainly substantial when it comes to sexuality, despite the sameness of the principles involved.

For example, one of the Protestants' main planks of the argument against the Catholic Church was the consideration that the sexual morality of the Church of Rome was too influenced by what was termed at the time laxity and dishonesty almost throughout its history.

This was, of course, a very easy criticism to level particularly at the time of the Reformation when prostitution was ignored and possibly even tolerated, if not encouraged, in Catholic countries. Sin was the principal manifestation of "the whore of Babylon" and consistently denounced by Protestantism as such.

The concept of confession, which will bring with it an absolution that may encourage the penitent to start again, seemed to be a contributory factor to a broad Catholic tolerance of sexual immorality. The punishments inflicted in England on those found guilty of sodomy or adultery in the 16th and 17th centuries (exile, imprisonment, whipping, placing in stocks and sometimes even stoning to death) are symptomatic of what one could term an enthusiastic frame of mind, which only began to moderate in the 18th and 19th centuries.

Whilst it must be admitted that the type of religious intolerance which followed on from the Reformation right through to the Edwardian period, and which has not entirely disappeared, has certainly lost much of its impact, and whilst it must also be acknowledged that as a result of more libertarian thinking Christianity appears to have lost much ground to other forms of belief, which, at least in England, border on Satanism, it is a fact that restrictions on sexual behaviour and performance imposed by religious tenets and fostered from an early age in both boys and girls can cause problems in adult life. It would be invidious to provide prurient examples of the point being made but those readers who have some experience of the world will no doubt see its relevance.

Centuries of uneven and occasionally cruel treatment of what was considered deviant behaviour as well as of varied punishment for sexual so-called misdemeanours have inevitably had an impact on our psychological make-up.

When it comes to our sexual instincts, much more than in any other field of human activity, the importance of our psychological heritage is paramount. In no way can it be discounted, let alone ignored: where we do, we act at our own peril and, as Jung so pithily put it, we finish up being ambuscaded by our own instinctual reactions.

CHAPTER FIFTEEN – What's Wrong with Us?

So far, consideration has been given to the theory. An attempt must now be made to look at the practical aspects, endeavouring as much as possible to avoid vulgarity.

The best description this writer can give of our approach to sex is to say that it is confused and severely constrained by a history of alternating phases of strict and often cruel retribution for immorality and adultery. Such confusion and constraint are genetic, aggravated by damp weather and grey skies and compounded by an uneven historical, cultural, religious and educational background.

Our cure for it, obviously, is to find a "laxative", namely alcohol, commonly relied upon to provide some kind of spontaneity and psychological freedom.

It should be made clear that the choice of such a cure is not exclusively English since most northern people (same weather conditions) are inclined to favour it. However, therein lies the uselessness of the remedy since it is common knowledge (except for the English male) that alcohol heightens the desire but dramatically reduces the performance, to the obvious dissatisfaction of one's female partner.

(For the sake of keeping some kind of balance, I should perhaps say, as a life-long wine imbiber, as used to be remarked in olden times, 'where Bacchus is absent, Venus waxes cold'. But then I suppose it is inevitably, and unfortunately, a fact that where alcohol is concerned excitement is not matched by performance...)

It must be admitted that this feature is clearly more relevant for the male than for the female, though it is arguable that a woman who has drunk too much is less able to appreciate and enjoy sex than her more sober sister (if only the poor young women who regularly get drunk on Saturday nights could understand this message!).

One is entitled to ask what are the signs of such confusion and constraints, which can at times amount to a form of psychological "constipation"? Here are a few instances, firstly by reference to the male.

Before considering them, however, it is worth recalling that there is at least another one of our traits which is the result of a related form of psychological constraint. The extent to which this comes about has often been ascribed to the English public school system, which, as a continental writer (Alexis de Tocqueville) observed nearly two centuries ago, is better at strengthening the mind than at broadening it. By this I mean the combination of strict discipline and chapel which cause restraint and a bottling up of feeling that is said to have been conducive to a war-like inclination that resulted in the establishment of the British Empire.

It really has not sufficed for E M Forster to object strongly to such English habit of bottling up one's feelings.

Indeed the Victorians expected women to exercise the same restraint that they practically demanded of men, to support men in doing so and, it was said, to stop them falling apart.

It wasn't for women to offer their men mere tea and sympathy.

Writing in 1872 ("The Expressions of the Emotions in Man and Animals") Charles Darwin – comparing the situation that prevailed in certain parts of the Continent – had observed that "Englishmen rarely cry, except under the pressure of the acutest grief". Whatever may have been the position at the time of Darwin, things are clearly changing nowadays given the frequency of English men crying in public. Indeed, the 2012 Olympics with their protracted manifestations of emotion expressed in tears, in public, especially on TV screens, by athletes (winners and losers), sports writers and TV interviewers are proof of the changes that are occurring in our society (interestingly, perhaps, many more men were pictured in tears than women; which goes to prove – if confirmation were really needed – that women are the stronger sex!).

It should be added that there is nothing novel about these recent manifestations of emotion since over the past 20 years or so British forms of address and of greetings have changed. Before it was a mere handshake, even assuming that one wanted to provide some kind of bodily contact by way of greeting. Nowadays, we have embraces and kisses on either one cheek or both and sometimes the exercise is repeated. It is often said that the greeting of a person, male or female, by kissing on the cheeks is the distinguishing feature of some cultures from the list of which the English were, until recently, excluded. Perhaps it is the effect of our having joined the European Union.

Difficult to determine what has happened to the stiff upper lip of the English (namely our concern not to display our emotions and our resistance to suffering and injuries) upon which Georgian society was bent and of which indeed it was proud. However, there is no doubt that it has gone.

It may well be that by giving public vent to our emotions, we are all becoming slightly more human...: if that is so, it is possible that greater emotion will provide a better impulse to our sexual performance! One wonders how, if he were around to witness such emotional outbursts by his compatriots, Darwin would react in assessing it in terms of his theory of evolution. Are we becoming more or less fit for survival by being more emotional? Comments, please, to the author with a SAE.

The average Englishman usually finds relations with the opposite sex difficult, if not frightening: that cramps his style, well apart from provoking, as an overreaction, a more than occasional tendency to use violence towards his woman. A further point is that the Englishman's lovemaking techniques are questionable, if the experience with agony aunts in newspapers and women's magazines is to be taken at face value. It is a fact that most English women when interviewed complained of their sex partner's lack of foreplay and of his clumsiness. Furthermore, in the little foreplay that occurs, the man is said to be either over-zealous or insensitive, recalling to mind the apt description of man in intercourse given by the French writer, Balzac, as an orang-utan trying to play the violin (apologies for the repetition, but it is quite an appropriate similitude; my fellow men may not like it but I am confident that most sensible and perceptive women will see its merit).

The Englishman is hesitant about taking the initiative where women are concerned, lest he should be rebuffed. By no means an unusual feature is that a group of boys visiting a pub is more likely than not to congregate near the bar or the dartboard than to care for female friends who are left on their own to gossip but, above all, to reflect on the uselessness of the male of the species. A similar situation, though perhaps not strictly related to sexual activity but more to social structure, used to occur amongst the upper classes in the 18th and 19th centuries when, after dinner, women were expected to retire to the drawing room leaving the men to cigars, port and... evacuation.

Our natural gregariousness, which until recently has served the country in good stead in war, in creating an empire and in establishing a cohesive, tolerant society is usually put forward to explain away this particular kind of situation; but that is only part of the story.

Of course, an Englishman feels that he must have sex: that is only natural. But the sooner it is over and done with, the more quickly he can pass on to something more interesting or at least psychologically less taxing eg. cricket, football, rugby etc. Such an approach can be troublesome for relationships since, contrary to what many people – especially of the Latin type – quite often believe, the English woman can be passionate and demanding, all the more so since the introduction of the contraceptive pill, a development which has created a different mood as well as more varied patterns of sexual behaviour in our country.

The average Englishman is rather puzzled about his sexuality. He seems to consider sex as something not really essential, possibly superficial, perhaps rather demeaning, if not dirty, and thus finds it difficult to distinguish between love and lust: even when he does, impossible to reconcile the two. Hence his need to "ennoble" the sexual feeling by romantic notions: as already observed above, it is not entirely a coincidence that the romantic movement in English poetry started in an English churchyard (apologies for the repetition...).

The resultant confusion between love and lust is at the root of most of the problems he experiences in his sexual, if not social, life; one of its major drawbacks is his inability to identify the nature of the woman with whom he comes into contact.

All too often a number of Englishmen tend to associate or become entangled with women who, for one reason or another, are not deserving of their attentions even when they are not quite clearly of easy virtue. This seems particularly true of public figures, especially footballers and politicians. Examples are too abundant to be listed here and, in any case, would be somewhat outside the scope of this exercise. The hungry Press, desperate to boost circulation by titillating the more than willing reading public, encouraged by those whose sole concern is shamefully to profit from such conduct by writing memoirs, giving interviews and immodestly providing humiliating information rich in intimate details, must bear a great responsibility for this situation.

One of the many sexual problems of English public figures is that very often they are not aware of how their sexuality affects their public countenance and the performance of their duties. Many a relationship, which is established by those who represent us in Government with public relation firms, journalists and their own staff and others seeking help from the Government in one form or the other, suffers from a hidden psychological subjection of man to woman.

One wonders how many initiatives are taken at government level which are influenced by leanings which are neither political nor patriotic; how many of those who govern us are forced to make concessions giving in to blackmail because of their sexual indiscretions or other scabrous behaviour; how many decisions are taken, benefits granted, contracts awarded, promotions set in train simply because of a significant look, the display of an actress's breast, of a chorus girl's legs or even willing posteriors.

In this kind of situation it is undoubted that other nationalities do not necessarily behave in the same manner; the French, for example, are usually more open about indiscretions despite the vagaries of their privacy laws, the Italians more tolerant despite the still noticeable strength of the family bond, the Spaniards more indifferent. Many Continentals seem to suffer less than the English from what one might be tempted to call sexual laissez-faire.

It is, of course, unfair – indeed presumptuous – to tar a whole people with the same brush!

There must obviously be Englishmen who by their behaviour in the bedroom and elsewhere can justify the claim of being God's gift to women; but if one has to judge from what one's friends, male and female, report or from what is regularly mentioned in newspapers and books – and nowadays increasingly on TV – our heterosexual relations are not too satisfactory.

The English male is more likely to look upon them as a duty and almost solely as a physical release rather than as a source of joy and of laughter, as stern in his deportment as the architecture of northern cathedrals. This is not to say that he cannot joke about sex; indeed, he does, frequently and loudly so, when it comes to the smuttiness of the 'Carry On' type of films or the seaside postcards. But how many can truly say that they also laugh about it in bed?

Unfortunately, it is almost impossible to justify statistically the statements being made. The mind boggles at the thought of the kind of questionnaire that would have to be sent out to millions of people... and one must leave the reader to come to his own conclusions.

----- oOo -----

It may not be entirely inappropriate at this stage, by way of confirmation of the fact that there must be something wrong with our sexual relations, to record statistical information published on April 4th 2012 and obtained by the NSPCC from police forces in England and Wales, as well as from the findings of the British Crime Survey, to the effect that in England and Wales between April 2010 and March 2011 there were over 23,000 sex offences against children under the age of 18.

Such offences covered the rape of a female child under 16 (5,115 in number), rape of a male child under 16 (918), offences of sexual assault on a female child under 13 (4,301), offences of sexual assault on a male child under 13 (1,125), of sexual activity involving a child under 16 (5,806) and of abuse of children through prostitution and pornography (152) plus 310 offences of sexual grooming.

As if that did not suffice, 38% of all rapes recorded by the police in England and Wales in the same period were committed against children under 16 years of age, 17,727 sexual crimes were recorded in total against children under 16 and 32% of the total of sexual crimes recorded in England and Wales (54,982) were against children under 16.

Perhaps the title of this book should be changed to the English and Sexual Crimes Against Children.

In common with most Western males (for reasons which are too numerous and complicated to be mentioned here) modern English man is experiencing increasing problems with his erectility. It is hardly surprising that this phase of relative impotence coincides with an extraordinary increase in the sale of sexual aids, to which reference has already been made, as well as of performance-enhancing medication.

A further factor that causes problems in heterosexual relations are the recent developments that have created a category of men, which hasn't really been analysed in great detail, if at all, whom one might call 'castrated'. Such category embraces all those men who, whether as fathers, lovers or partners, find themselves under psychological pressure because of the fact that modern woman is (a) freely available and (b) in the ascendant.

To understand this category it is necessary to make a slight digression. Assuming Darwin is right, it is a fact that man has developed over millennia as the hunter and the fighter of the species, whereas woman has been concerned primarily with procreation. As a result man has developed bigger muscles and a much more violent fighting instinct to enable him to assert himself and provide food for which his mate was grateful and for which she may even have forgiven him being dragged by the hair into a cave!

These fairly primitive representations of early men and women are not necessarily to be believed but one cannot deny the physical and psychological truth that man, throughout history, has had to hunt both for food and for sex.

Accordingly, man has developed as the head of the family because he was the breadwinner, as the father and the protector of the family because that was his role, as the lord and master of the manor and the hunter for food and women.

For whatever reason, and it would take too long to investigate this aspect of the matter, nowadays very often woman is the principal if not the real breadwinner.

It is admittedly a fact that man found it easy to settle down to being a mere father and for quite a while he managed to get away with it. Nowadays, however, man himself has brought about the demise of such function since we can so easily provide woman with a child, not only without the physical presence of a father but even without knowing who the father is or was, since men are prepared to bequeath their seed for posterity. This disposes very easily of the sexual aspect of being a father.

Furthermore the State is replacing him in all his functions gradually, but inevitably and more and more people, especially women, are relying upon it rather than upon a man to support them and their children.

By the same token man can no longer be looked upon as the protector of his woman and his family since we now have the National Health Service, the Social Services, the Local Authority, the Police, etc. Indeed, nowadays any father is at serious risk of breaking the law if he even spanks his children let alone caresses his daughter; and if we were to consider, cynically, any possible financial benefit accruing to his family from his presence, it is probably true to say that in most middle class families of the Western world mother and children would be infinitely better off financially if the father were dead rather than alive, either because of the payments to be made by his employers under pension schemes (nowadays at a reducing rate) or through individually maintained insurance.

It is a fact that if a father does earn a good income then, particularly in certain strata of Western society, he may be able to provide his children with special advantages (like private education or equivalent benefits) but the difficulty remains that there is doubt about his present day economic utility. That this is true finds endorsement in the fact that there are many more women who have children as a matter of choice without either marrying or cohabiting with man. The number of such women is increasing all the time.

More importantly, however, man's hunting instinct has practically disappeared. By which is here meant the basic need to kill or use violence in order to survive and to use force in order to obtain sexual satisfaction, even though he may still have to struggle to assert and prove himself vis-á-vis his colleagues in business, in the professions or on the factory floor. But the hunting instinct is very powerful and it has been dulled almost into insensitivity by the fact that man no longer needs to hunt in order to satisfy his sexual proclivities since women are exceptionally ready and willing – through their emancipation admittedly but, above all, through reliable contraception controlled by them – to offer their sexual partnership whether on a casual or on a more permanent basis.

It seems quite clear that recent social and scientific developments have resulted in some emasculation of man, to put it at its lowest.

It is no concern of this booklet to analyse the effect that the disappearance of the concept of man as a father will have upon woman (let alone deleteriously upon children). There is an argument that the intimacy in the relationship between mother and father stemming from the cooperation needed in rearing the children is totally unrelated to sexual relations per se and is of fundamental importance for the well-being of the child, his emotional and educational development and his function as a useful, honest and hard-working member of society.

Such intimacy cannot be replaced by any other sort of set up. Its principal significance is to ensure the psychological stability of the children existing in the nuclear family as traditionally understood and, as such, is of paramount importance. (But of itself this consideration may not necessarily be relevant to sexual performance.)

Nevertheless, it is probably worthwhile quoting hereunder a set of statistics published by the Organisation for Economic Cooperation and Development in 2007, which show that out of

30 countries considered, worldwide, the United Kingdom lies 27th in the percentage of children aged up to 14 who live in the same household as both their parents, namely 68.9%. In 26th place, with a percentage of 70.7%, we find the United States (a rather sad commentary on the two main English-speaking nations, whose sexual behaviour and deviations seem to run along parallel lines).

This should be compared with Finland (95.2%), Greece (93.6%), and Italy (92.1%).

It is here left to psychologists to consider what the effect of the absence of the father is on the children (possible feminisation for the boys, possible disrespect for a father figure – and as a result for man generally – as far as the girls are concerned).

The table below, taken from the Daily Mail of December 29th 2012, is fairly indicative:

The Stability League

Percentage of Children aged up to 14 who live in the same household as both their parents

1	Finland	95.2	17	Switzerland	84.7
2	Greece	93.6		OECD AVERAGE	84.1
3	Italy	92.1	18=	Germany	82
4=	Luxembourg	91.5	18=	Hungary	82
4=	Spain	91.5	18=	Poland	82
4=	Turkey	91.5	21	Denmark	81.3
7	Malta	90	22	Czech Republic	80.8

8	Romania	88.9	23	France	79.5
9=	Japan	87.7	24	Sweden	78
9=	Slovenia	87.7	25	Lithuania	72.4
11	Netherlands	87.4	26	United States	70.7
12	Mexico	87.1	27	**United Kingdom**	**68.9**
13=	Austria	86.6	28	Estonia	66.8
13=	Portugal	86.6	29	Belgium	65
15	Slovakia	86.4	30	Latvia	64.9
16	Bulgaria	85.2			

Source: Organisation for Economic Co-Operation and Development.
Figures relate to 2007, the most recent comparable figures.

Furthermore, we should not forget that man has handed over to the State absolute control over those who threaten his family; he had long ago renounced his duty and privilege of feeding and clothing his children when Welfare Services were established ready to take over at any time – indeed, all too often – where he might be deficient; he abdicated from his position of master when he invented the contraceptive pill, which enabled woman alone to control her reproductive function; he converted himself into a non-entity as far as procreation is concerned at the stage when his own scientific advantages enabled sperm to be preserved for posterity; he surrendered his pride, his prestige and his inheritance at the same time as he began to find his fellow men more interesting and acceptable than his women.

A combination of these three factors: namely contraception, man's greed to profit from new inventions and his ever-decreasing masculinity, all occurred in effect within the last 100 years in England but at an ever-accelerating speed over the past 20 years or so.

We should not be puzzled therefore that nowadays man sits back and watches pornographic and violent films where he sees displayed the kind of violence that he finds more and more difficult to officially and lawfully indulge in himself. He is effectively frustrated because his mind has become disordered and that's when his frustration often turns to violence, assuming he can still find sufficient strength to overcome his passivity. Such frustration inevitably affects his sexual drive and erectility.

People react in surprise and despair when they hear of manifestations of inexplicable and totally unwarranted violence, particularly of a sexual kind. Some even turn round and determine that it is only man – as opposed to woman – who is capable of being a criminal; others argue that in a world run by women such violence would not exist; there may be some who feel that perhaps all men should be castrated! (But preserving, please, a few milligrams of seed for use if required.)

All this may sound like an exaggeration, which of course it is, but is an attempt to focus the reader's imagination on the development of modern English man's psyche; of the man who may want to use an element of gentle force and violence within a sexual context, remnants possibly of a more basic and all-pervasive hunting instinct for which he can longer find a natural outlet.

It is here suggested that the ease with which modern English woman surrenders herself has a deleterious effect on her mate's masculinity; indeed – it must be repeated – on his erectility. One should say that the excitability of man as a result of woman's not-so-easy availability improves his sexual performance. It remains true, as our forefathers believed, that woman's modesty is a strong factor in the excitability of man. We appear to have forgotten the old saying that there is more pulling power in a single pubic hair than in a fully-masted brigantine!

Furthermore, we in England are also increasingly ignoring the well-established psychological fact that in the sexual relationship between a man and a woman, the less the man sees, the more he wants to see.

There was certainly more excitement for him years ago in seeing a few inches of a woman's calf than in having splashed before his eyes, by films and TV programmes, images of full frontal female nudity, which leave nothing to the poor man's imagination, which in turn becomes denuded.

No studies have apparently been made as to the consequences of the ease with which young girls grant sexual favour, especially intercourse, to boys has on them and on society.

We have already recorded the suggestion that such ease provides no outlet for man's hunting instinct. He is deprived of the need to expend energy, to display the charm, blandishments, technique, even perhaps the 'force' (by which I mean, of course, not violence, but 'gentle' persuasion) that nature has endowed him with to conquer a prey for as such, deep down in his subconscious, he still considers a woman when he is motivated solely be instinct rather than by love.

The question does not appear to have been asked as to where those energies, especially in young men, will be redirected. The probability is that they will be diverted to reactions, often of a sexual nature, towards other women or the society of which the youngster very often feels he is not part. Such ease in this writer's opinion may well explain the ever-increasing manifestations of heartless, mindless, capricious, incomprehensible brutality and violence.

Another factor which tends to aggravate our confusion about sexual activity is our fondness for the understatement, of which we, English men and women, are said to be masters.

To say to someone who has consciously told an untruth 'you are mistaken' rather than 'you are a liar' is obviously less controversial and makes for a less contentious debate. So far, no real harm done save that the statement lacks cogency.

But to use regularly the term 'paedophile' (linguistically correct and sounding more elegant) instead of 'child abuser' or 'child molester' is to hide the true significance of the conduct of which complaint is being made.

The prefix or suffix 'phil-e' derives from the Greek to like or to be fond of. It usually denotes (except possibly for philander/er) a favourable, dignified activity (philately, philosophy, philanthropy, philharmonic). It is not merely confusing but wrong to use it as a noun that describes the abuse of children.

Our tendency to adopt words or expressions which relate to conduct or activities which can be unpleasant is one of the major failings of modern English language and society. Good old-fashioned descriptions are no longer preferred: we seem to have been all brainwashed into applying wrong definitions or using words which are superficially more pleasant.

In similar fashion, those who come to the end of their lives because they have drunk too much are now said to have died because of alcohol poisoning; no longer alcohol abuse. It is as though by changing words we have relieved the person from responsibility for their conduct.

The prostitute is more often a call-girl, the dustbin man a refuse collector, a flat in Kentish Town becomes an apartment on the Côte d'Azur. What we seem to have forgotten is George Orwell's 'Newspeak' and the well-known argument by Sir Francis Bacon that it is words that control us rather than the reverse.

Similarly, a number of nouns and adjectives used until 20 years ago to describe homosexual activity are now almost universally converted into 'gay', which gives a tone of cheerfulness to a particular type of conduct.

There has now been occurring, for many years, a psychological manipulation in the use of our English language, which is often believed to be coincidental. However, sometimes one has to wonder whether it is right to describe idiomatic changes as an evolution of the language rather than artificially produced terminological pollution.

Turning now in greater detail to the English woman, one should make a general observation, which is also applicable to the English man and which endorses the point made above about the need for an alcoholic, sexual stimulant to remedy the "constipation": this is our inordinate fondness for partying and boozing, our need for a catalyst to our emotion.

Whether it be a birthday party, a marriage party, a bottle party, a Christmas party or the all-embracing office party, little seems to appeal more to English people, and especially English women, than going to a festive event where alcohol will be freely available as a matter of course. This is a well-established fact. It is at parties that one can let one's hair down, as the expression goes; the more alcohol consumed there, the more successful the celebration.

An English woman, no matter how mature, even more than her man, thinks of nothing more enjoyable than going out to a party. Gone are the days when she had to stay at home darning the socks of her husband or her children: at long last, she is free to enjoy herself. Tea and sympathy have been replaced by alcohol and sex.

The younger women feel exactly the same. It has been written somewhere that young English girls of today no longer take their teddy bear to bed but a bottle of beer. This may sound extreme but certain forms of behaviour even in public places are clear evidence that the statement may not be quite so far-fetched as it appears at first blush.

Such never-ending search for what are, in reality, outlets for sexuality is another aspect of the obsession that colours the approach to sex of English people generally.

This is, of course, a generalisation but it is less extreme than might appear at first reading. Certainly the images of English women that are projected in newspapers and on television in present times very often do not differ too dramatically from the description given above.

Secondly, one should note that practically every year in the UK 41,000 children are born to unmarried girls under the age of 18. Indeed, information published on December 14th 2010 records that the UK has the highest and fastest growing rate of illegitimacy in Europe. This is hardly surprising since it is common knowledge – though most of us prefer to ignore it – that English young girls are quite precocious and, indeed, promiscuous.

There seems to be little doubt that, at least in modern times, this willingness to indulge in sexual activity prior to or outside marriage can be said to have started during World War II when it was brought about by two significant factors.

In the first place, women were forced to become more emancipated as they replaced men for the war effort. Working in factories, on farms, in government departments and generally proving their worth encouraged independence of mind and a greater sense of freedom.

Secondly, the temptations provided by the then numerous American soldiers based in Britain, at a time when rationing was in force, proved too strong to resist. Cigarettes, KP rations, “Smartie” type chocolates, plenty of spending money and, above all, silk stockings were an understandable inducement to a liberalisation of sexual mores.

These tempting features were not only well received by single women. In the same manner in which the rate of divorce rose after the 1914-18 war, the percentage of divorce petitions on the grounds of adultery rose when the Second World War was over; two-thirds of the immediately post-war divorces being initiated by husbands as the rate of divorce proceedings 'rocketed'. It is more than a mere suggestion to state that the prime cause was wartime wifely infidelity[20].

As we have already observed, nowadays, English women are willing to renounce their virginity at an increasingly early age since it is not unusual for them to start having intercourse as young as 14 and sometimes at 12 years of age.

The decrease in the age of first intercourse is very noticeable indeed (some figures have already been provided). Women born between 1931 and 35 on average had their first experience of intercourse aged 21; for women born between 1936 and 1940 the age fell to 20 and for those born between 41 and 45 it had dropped to 19.

Women born between 1966 and 75 experienced first intercourse at the age of 17 but since the '90s, as observed, that age has fallen steadily.

---

[20] *v. Lawrence Stone, Road to Divorce 1530-1987, Oxford University Press, 1990, p401*

In passing, one should observe that there has been an equally dramatic decrease in the age at which boys and girls have their first sexual experience (as distinct from intercourse) the median age dropping from 16 to 14 for women and 15 to 13 for men so that it is quite clear that a sizeable majority of young people are now sexually active before the age of 16.

In addition to the information provided by the Kinsey Reports (v. above) statistics have been produced to show that 18.7% of women aged 16-19 most definitely have experienced sexual intercourse before the age of 16 compared with fewer than 1% of those aged 55-59 (the equivalent proportion for men being 27.6% and 5.8%)[21].

It is here suggested that there is a close correlation between vulgar thoughts and vulgar speech. A psychiatrist who applied his mind to this situation would certainly realise that not only has the use of four letter words by young girls dramatically increased, as already observed above, but also one notices a remarkable use of vulgar or unnecessarily offensive expressions of the kind which certainly the older generation would find rather difficult to accept, let alone understand. Of course, older

---

[21] *National Survey of Sexual Attitudes and Lifestyle in England, Kaye Wellings, Julia Field, Ann Johnson and Jane Wadsworth with Sally Bradshaw in Penguin Books, London 1994*

people have always complained about younger ones and there is nothing new in the changes in language. As George Elliot (Mary Anne Evans) had observed in her novel Romola (published in 1863) already in her times women spoke 'with much uncomplimentary remonstrance in terms remarkably identical with the insults in use by the gentler sex of the present day...' But there is an argument for maintaining that rude or vulgar expressions or words don't sit comfortably on the mouths of women, especially young ones.

One further observation as regards the English woman: the grimace of orgasm is no substitute for an expression of joy and humour before and/or after intercourse; or so at least it is understood in this work.

There seems little doubt that English women of the 18th century were much more active, joyful, sentimental and sexy and despite the greater concern of Georgian society for a strong depiction of family life as appears particularly in the paintings of Johan Zoffany, probably continued to be playful throughout the century.

It may be interesting to revert to the most troublesome modern feature, however, concerning the sexual behaviour of young

English girls and women and that is the ease with which they indulge in sexual intercourse regardless of age.

It is as though intercourse was something that had to be experienced at the earliest moment regardless of any feeling of real desire or tenderness, let alone love, and no matter really with whom.

This easy, almost casual abandonment and lack of discernment brings to mind the occasional, hyperbolic and absurdly misogynistic observation by some Latin men that women would even lie with donkeys but for concern for their bed sheets...!

Far-fetched, of course, as well as unfair; misogyny is on the increase whatever we may wish to think.

-------------------- oOo ---------------------

Before trying to forecast whether the present-day attitude to sex of the English people which has, particularly in the past few decades, started to undergo very important changes, is likely to develop in different and perhaps more successful directions, a short digression seems appropriate.

The English are, obviously, an island people. As islanders we have developed to a very marked degree the ability to close ranks against foreigners and invaders but, above all, to do so when criticised. As islanders, we have also developed a keen sense of superiority and our insularity has in fact forged our way of thinking and of behaving through the ages: the creation of the British Empire is proof of this fact. There has thus come about what has become known as the 'great British character' namely the resilience in the face of adversity and the ability to overcome problems at a national level even if very often one has to 'muddle through'. Some of the cartoons of the magazine *Punch* vividly display features of such national traits, a classic being the vignette of the four bridge players in evening dress under a tent in the desert.

This closing of ranks, this ability to sacrifice even one's individuality for the common good, has proved a boon historically and a very good feature politically. It has however a serious drawback: namely, the tendency to be over-sensitive about criticism especially when coming from non-English people, and more particularly, to reject outright without due consideration any objection that may be made to the English way of life. That drawback has proved to have serious social consequences and interestingly enough has become much more noticeable as the country has grown less significant in world history, having lost an Empire and, some might argue, its sense of historical direction.

Practically gone are observations by the English people about themselves based on caricature, satire and self-criticism, exception made perhaps for the magazine Private Eye. On the contrary, we have started looking at ourselves through rose-tinted glasses, failing completely to realise that in social terms we may be standing close to the edge of a precipice.

No, not even rose-tinted: our glasses are darkened. What prevails nowadays is a desire not to face up to or to look at the truth of our problems. The primary motivating force of the English in the past two decades or so has become the totally absurd sentimentality to which we are all addicted. It is sentimentality which has taken the place of truth. The judgements we make of situations and of problems are no longer inspired by our centuries-old common sense but by this wonderful, reasonably novel addition to our intellect and to our emotions, sentimentality. It is strange: we who have always condescendingly and very critically ascribed sentimentality to the Latins now find ourselves enslaved by it. (Just consider the emotional storm generated by the death of Princess Diana.)

Sentimentality is not conducive to good judgement. When it comes to our sexual relations, it is deleterious because it prevents us from distinguishing clearly between black and white: our sexual relations then tend to fall into the category of grey in the sense that nothing is definite, nothing is clear, every shade of colour and of conduct is tolerated since it relieves us of responsibility for passing judgement. Indeed, it is often awkward to determine whether sentimentality is or is not more damaging than non-judgmentalism, and it is almost a chicken-and-egg situation to determine which of the two comes first.

This attitude is combined with one of extreme hope. Even where we see the impropriety or the evil around us, we hope that by not confronting it, it will go away. It isn't even a matter of sweeping it under the carpet: sweeping something under the carpet requires action, movement, a decision to eliminate something. We are becoming incapable even of doing that: we prefer to let things slide, encouraged by a passive, despondent attitude, which is not really English.

Apart from occasional deviations, more and more significant has become the application of the motto 'right or wrong, my country' (we no longer remember what G K Chesterton had to say about this maxim, namely 'my mother, drunk or sober').

There is a refusal to discuss our sexual failings even though sex appears to be the only topic of conversation. As far as we the English are concerned, all is fine in our sexual world.

There is a narrow-mindedness about this attitude, which recalls Napoleon's description of the English (which he borrowed from Adam Smith) as 'a nation of shopkeepers'.

'Muddling through' is of no use whatever – indeed, is positively dangerous – where children, crime and sexual affairs are concerned, situations in which a 'moral' or statement of principle and policy is essential.

It is conceivable that in one or two generations' time we may see an overall improvement in English sexual relations; what is almost certain is there will be a much greater variety of behaviour because as our political and economic freedoms diminish, sexual freedom will inevitably tend to compensate for such loss by its increase. Furthermore, it is probable that we shall all have learnt much more about sexuality generally, as well as about the relevant techniques, from the ever-increasing mass of texts of one kind or the other dedicated to them by the internet, newspapers, TV programmes and by women's magazines.

Not to be discounted is the possibility that just as we have developed drugs like Viagra, Cialis and Levitra to aid men suffering from erectile dysfunction so we may in the not too distant future discover a single-dose tablet, which will have the ability to infuse into the English male a great sense of amorousness, if one may be forgiven for using that expression, which will improve his lovemaking generally.

A further important fact may well be the influx of other people and the admixture of races which is occurring in the UK and which is altering the face of the country. Coupled with the increase of foreign travel, which may provide a better, if not too different, education, there are a few signs of improvement. There are also abundant graphic representations and a wealth of “technical” details often of extreme pruriency bordering on the pornographic, that our youngsters may be able to extract, especially from the internet, and indeed, may be forgiven for realising that sex is anything but a kind of clockwork orange. On the other hand, maybe not, since a vital spark will probably always be missing if English weather conditions remain unaltered...; in any event, it will not be easy to bring improvement to our sexual thinking and performance whilst the degree, ever-increasing, of our coarseness of thought, manners and conduct remains at its current level.

Also worthy of note is the fact that those of us who, whether for reasons of personal morality, religious belief, social conscience, concern for our families and the future of our children and grandchildren, or whatever, feel the responsibility – if not the need – to draw attention to the present and, more importantly, the future consequences of beliefs and conduct of the kind which have been mentioned above (perhaps all too often...), are invariably met with a refusal to acknowledge the problems. We are usually contradicted by answers along the lines: "the public are not interested in such things", "the public don't want know".

A final difficulty that we shall have to face is the fact that over the past two decades or so, there has developed in a good percentage of the British people a sense of concern, if not of real fear, about speaking one's own mind, as recent developments regarding the conspiracy of silence about particular types of offences, especially against children, have come to light after many years. There must be some situations of the type described where the average English man (and woman) would be tempted to exclaim: enough!; might be tempted to express dissent from views which are claimed to be generally accepted by the public at large or from behaviour which is considered unpleasant; but the voices that could be raised in criticism, if not in opposition, to many forms of sexual behaviour, which we now take for granted in our society, are often not even heard, for the simple reason that we are afraid to advertise them to the world at large even when occasionally we speak about them in rather muted terms.

Equally significant and damaging is our fear that in either criticising or revealing certain types of sexual – and other – conduct we would not be believed, that we could not penetrate the barrier erected around certain types of activities, which ought to be publicised rather than hidden from view.

We are afraid that we might be accused of not being with it, of not understanding modern behaviour, of being 'old fogies' incapable of moving with the times. These accusations are as twisted and false as they are often naive and dishonest. Above all, however, they are dangerous for they bar the way to the ascertainment of the true social consequences of certain kinds of conduct.

The outcome, highly damaging for society and morality, as well as for the administration of justice, is the establishment of a sexual mafia where, Sicilian-style, silence about deviant sexual conduct is guaranteed by a code of dishonour, which is quite un-English; and which is proving as hard to eradicate as its criminal or political counterpart. Whistleblowers are dismissed, pilloried or even prosecuted.

As a result, we keep our views to ourselves, concerned that if we were permitted (a big if...) to publicise them, we would be liable to attack. Perhaps not physically attacked in the real sense, although even that could not be excluded given the violent nature of our social behaviour, but hit by a mass onslaught of the Press or others in a position of power.

I suppose it is not too much to say that when it comes to matters relating to those parts of our anatomies, which until recently were kept reasonably well covered but nowadays are on open display, the English turn themselves into ostriches: they bury their heads in the sand.

That is sad.

But enough complaining: I have no desire to be lynched!

CHAPTER SIXTEEN - CONCLUSION

It must by now have become apparent to the reader that the view has been adopted here that, for one reason or the other, the male of the species is weakening and that is one of the principal reasons why we are in such a sexual mess.

True, he is still of use in making wars and in committing abuses of one kind or the other; of proving that cruelty and stupidity are almost entirely his modern prerogative; of failing in his duties to his family and to society as a whole. But his importance is diminishing and some people may maintain, with a degree of justification, that he appears to be in the process of exhausting his historical function.

If this be right and if it be correct that the 'rehabilitation' of woman is continuing on a daily basis, it may be appropriate to conclude on a rather 'feminist' note by considering how she has developed in English society.

In a book of this nature, which relates in the main to sexual activity, it would be inappropriate to provide any kind of history of the English woman's development through the centuries, although such an exercise would be useful for a better understanding not only of herself but also of her man. After all, it is only by knowing any woman of a different nationality or race that one can have a better understanding of the man of her same origin. Her tendencies should be his desires, her passions his failings, her dissatisfaction his uselessness.

It will suffice to remark that gone are the days when the English woman had no rights, could not make a contract or a will, could not hold property nor incur debts and could not divorce her husband.

The path trodden by woman from the 16th century to modern days has been too well documented by historians, sociologists and writers generally to require further comment but it may be interesting to observe very briefly the various stages in which English woman found herself over the past 300 years.

Not much can be stated with any degree of certainty about the sexual life of English women in the 17th and 18th centuries save to say that they must have had one.

Equally, there were marriages of one kind or the other, there was adultery, and children were born: life went on and there is nothing new there but the idea long prevailed that marriage was essentially for the purpose of procreation and, to some extent, especially amongst the nobility and the landed gentry, that woman should reach the altar untainted.

But to observe that we do not know much about the behaviour of our women in the past, starting, say, with the 17th century, is not strictly correct. It can be said that when the decade of Cromwell's control of society came to an end, English women had a period when they finally started to blossom.

Especially amongst the richer families, courtesans and ladies of the nobility became very well known and their names, and the same amount of gossip about them as we have nowadays concerning film stars, presenters and footballers' wives, appeared in a number of pamphlets. There were many of these as a result of the spread of printing. So much so that there was a very well-known pamphlet entitled 'The Observer' which contained what today we might call gossip. True enough, it was a publication controlled by men, just as male was its reading public and we don't know whether husbands showed the leaflets to their wives. Nevertheless, it is a fact that throughout the 25-year reign of Charles II, his courtesans acquired great power, not only emotional but also political. In fact there was published a pamphlet by prostitutes having the title "The Poor Whore's Petition" where they complained of the attention given to the courtesans. 'Pictures' and paintings of the king's various mistresses were very popular indeed.

It is also true that William III was less lax in his approach to women than Charles II and certainly did not approve of the fact that way back in 1660 his predecessor had reopened the theatres, which had been closed for the previous 20 years.

But there were women who did come to prominence. It is probably too much to call them the first feminists but there are three of them who are worthy of mention: namely Margaret Cavendish (Duchess of Newcastle), the very well-known Nell Gwynne and particularly Aphra Behn, the author who had the honour of being buried in Westminster Abbey.

But that is the past. We have learned much more about the English woman over the past 200 years.

One can thus summarise and conclude by saying that there are six highly significant dates in the history of English woman's emancipation especially by reference to sexual activity.

The first is 1857 when, at long last, Parliament decided that marriage was no longer for life and divorce, which until then had been officially available only in strict circumstances by act of Parliament to wealthy people, could become available for specific reasons both to men and to women.

The second date of great importance is 1882 when, after two previous unsatisfactory pieces of legislation in 1870 and 1875, the Married Women Property Act was passed, which abolished the submission, indeed the slavery, of woman to man. From that moment onwards man was no longer in control of his wife's property and women acquired rights, initially limited, to enter into contracts. In short, that Act was a major stepping stone for woman's emancipation from her husband; it still took some time for the more obvious inequalities between the sexes to be eliminated, for it was only in 1918, the third important date, that woman at long last obtained an almost unqualified right to vote (suffrage being made available to all women over the age of 30).

As already observed, 1961 was perhaps the most significant date in the sexual life of English women because then the contraceptive pill became available.

Six years later, the Abortion Act was passed, which gave woman the unfettered right to decide on the result of her sexual proclivities.

The last date, and socially as significant as 1961, was 1969 when the Divorce Reform Act was passed, which effectively made divorce available both to men and women on demand and thus brought to an end the reign of the family as traditionally understood.

Woman has made incredible strides forward towards emancipation and there is no point in arguing about the merit of such progress. It has more than once been observed that there is only one question to be asked at the end of the day: is woman any happier as a result?

The answer to the question, at least in the present writer's view, is no. One can debate to the point of sickness whether such a negative conclusion is correct but the least that can be said is that, correct or not, the chasm between the sexes and the hypocrisy with which it is viewed, is growing wider. This is so despite woman's complete legal and social equality; man's reducing masculinity does not help.

One is forced to the conclusion that the unsatisfactory nature of the relationship between man and woman, especially in a sexual context, appears to be congenital.

As Tolstoy so aptly put it: ‘man survives earthquakes, epidemics, the horrors of disease and all agonies of the soul but, for all time, his most tormenting tragedy has been, and is, and will be, the tragedy of the bedroom’.

Postscriptum

This work was completed just before the NSPCC published, on March 4th 2013, data which they had obtained under the Freedom of Information Act 2000 from the Police Authorities of 34 out of the 43 forces, which they had approached in England and Wales.

The figures are incomplete because the Authorities for the West Midlands, Greater Manchester and the London Metropolitan Police (the three largest in the UK) were either unable or unwilling to provide the information requested. From which one may deduce that the data provided represent a substantially smaller proportion of the total and could be said to be the tip of the iceberg.

Nevertheless, they're worth noting because they indicate that over the past three years there were more than 5,000 formal investigations into the behaviour of youngsters under 18 accused of crimes including rape and sexual assault.

They further show that the number of sex offences allegedly committed by under-18s has increased by 38% from 1,432 in 2009/10 to 1,978 in 2011/12 from which one can extrapolate that every day our police are dealing with at least five 'children' accused of sexual offences.

The data supplied by the Humberside, Cambridgeshire and Avon and Somerset forces show that the youngest cases of 'harmful sexual behaviour' had involved children aged five!

Overall, a total of 5,028 offences categorised as 'harmful sexual behaviour' were recorded between 2009 and 2012. The data supplied by all the forces that replied to the request for information show that 98% of the offenders were boys.

The author refrains from the obvious comment on the information thus elicited.

BIBLIOGRAPHY

LOOK AROUND!

You may however find some of the following texts useful.

Abse, Leo: *Fellatio, Masochism, Politics & Love*, Robson Books, London, 2000

Anderson, Digby: *The Loss of Virtue*, Social Affairs Unit, 1992

Aver A, Egenter R, O'Connor F: *Celibacy and Virginity*, Gill & Son, Dublin & Sidney, 1968.80.

Baker, Margaret: *Folklore and Customs of Rural England*, David & Charles, London 1974

Bardet, Jean Pierre: *La 1ere Fois, Ou, Le Roman De La Virginité Perdue A' Travers Les Siècles Et Les Continents*, Paris, Editions Ramsay, 1982

Bond, Stephanie: *About Last Night*, Richmond, Mills Boon, 2000

Bowman, Henry: *Marriage for Moderns*, New York, McGraw-Hill, 1965

Brandon, Ruth: *The New Women and the Old Men*, Secker & Warburg, London 1989

Briant, Keith: The Hogarth Press, 1962

Burgess, Ernest W: *Engagement and Marriage*, Philadelphia Lippincott 1953

Catullus, Carmina: as *The Poems of Catullus* trnsl., James Michie, Rupert Hart-Davis, London 1969

Chesser, Eustace: *Is Marriage Necessary?*, W H Allen, London, 1974

Christie, A J: St Ambrose (Bishop of Milan) – single works (De Virginibus), *On Holy Virginibus*, J H Parker, Oxford 1843

Cloudsley, Anne: *Women of Omdurman*, private edition 1981

Cooper, Kate: *The Virgin and the Bride*, Cambridge, Mass., Harvard University Press 1999

Dabhoiwala, Faramerz: *The Origins of Sex (A History of the First Sexual Revolution)*, Allen Lane, London, 2012

Dworkin, Andrea: *Intercourse*, Martin Secker & Warburg, London, 1987
Ellis, Albert: *Sex Without Guilt*, New York, Lyle Stewart 1958
Ellis, Havelock: *Studies on the Psychology of Sex (6 Vols)*, Heinemann, London, 1906
Foucault, Michel: *The Will to Knowledge*, The History of Sexuality Volume I, Alan Lane 1979
Freud, Sigmund: *Sexuality and the Psychology of Love*, Prentice Hall & IBD 1993
Friedan, Betty: *The Feminine Mystique*, Gollantz, London 1963
Goldhill, Simon: *Foucault's Virginity*, Cambridge Univ Press, New York 1995
Goodall, Richard: *The Comfort of Sin*, Renaissance Books, 1995
Gould, Davis: *Elizabeth in The First Sex* Putman, New York, 1971
Greer, Germaine: *The Female Eunuch*, 1970
Hilderbrand, Dietrich Von: *In Defence of Purity* (translation by J Kosel & F Pustet), Sheed & Ward, London, 1931
Holtzman, Deanna & Nancy Kulish: *Nevermore: the Hymen and the Loss of Virginity*, Northvale, N.J. J Aronson 1997
Huxley, Aldous: *Brave New World*, Harper & Rowe, N.Y. 1946
James, Oliver: *Britain on the Couch*, Century, London 1997
Johnson, M & Ryan, T: *Sexuality in Greek & Roman Society & Literature*, Routledge Taylor & Francis Group, Abingdon, Oxon, 2005
Kennedy, Helena: *Just Law – The Changing Face of Justice*, Chatto & Windus, London, 2004
Kinsey, A C & Others: *The Sexual Behaviour of the Human Female*, W B Saunders & Co, Philadelphia 1952
Kinsey, A C & Others: *The Sexual Behaviour of the Human Male*, W B Saunders & Co, Philadelphia, 1948
Laqueur, Thomas: *Making Sex (Body and Gender from the Greeks to Freud)*, Harvard University Press, Cambridge and London, 1990
Larkin, Philip: *Collected Poems*, The Marvell Press and Faber & Faber 1988
Lawrence, D H: *Lady Chatterley's Lover*, 1928

Locke, Harvey J: *Predicting Adjustment in Marriage*, Reinhard and Winston, New York 1951
Loughlin, Marie: *Hymeneutics : Interpreting Virginity on the Early Modern Stage*, Lewisburt, Bucknell Univ Press 1997
Mace, David: *Encyclopaedia of Sexual Behaviour*, New York Hawthorn Books 1961
Masters, W H and Johnson, V E: *Human Sexual Response*, New York 1966
McCarthy, Tara: *Been There, Haven't Done That – A Virgin's Memoir*, Warner Books, Little, N.Y., 1997
Meade, Margaret: *Male & Female*, Pelican, 1962
Michie, James: *The Poems of Catullus*, Gerald Duckworth & Co 1989
Millet, Kate: *Sexual Politics*, Virago Press, 1977
Montserrat, Dominic: *Sex and Society in Græco-Roman Egypt*, Kegan Paul Int, London 1996
Nin, Anais: *Little Birds – Erotica*, MacMillan, 1979
Paxman, Jeremy: *The English-A Portrait of A People*, Penguin Books, London, 1999
Perrin, Joseph Marie: *Virginity* (translated by K Gordon), Blackfriars Publications, London, 1956
Porter, Roy & Paul, Lesley *The Facts of Life – the Creation of Sexual Knowledge in Britain 1650-1950*, Yale University Press, 1995
Roberts, Andrew: *The Eminent Churchillians*, Phoenix, 1995
Russell, Bertrand: *Marriage & Morals*, Unwin Paperbacks, 1976
Schulenburg, Jane: Tibbetts *Forgetful of their Sex: Female Sanctity and Society*, Chicago, University of Chicago Press 1998
Seaman, Barbara: *Free and Female*, Coward McCann & Geoghegan Inc., New York, 1972
Shakespeare, William: *All's Well That Ends Well, Pericles*
Sloane, Ethel: *Biology of Women*, New York, Wiley & Sons, 1985
Spender, Dale: *Women Have Ideas*, Pandora, 1982
Steinem, Gloria: *Outrageous Acts and Everyday Rebellions*, 1983
Stone, Lawrence: *Road to Divorce 1530-1987*, Oxford University, 1990

Stopes, Mary: *Married Love*, The Hogarth Press, 1980
Stopes, Mary: *Wise Parenthood*, Putnam & Co, 1980
Travis, Alan: *Bound & Gagged – A Secret History of Obscenity in Britain*, Profile Books, London, 2000
Wellings Kaye, Field Julia, Johnson Ann, Wadsworth Bradshaw Sally: *National Survey of Sexual Attitudes & Lifestyle in England*, Penguin Books, London, 1994
Wilson, A N: *God's Funeral*, John Murray, London, 1999

Reports

BMJ Specialist Journals on 21 October 1999
John Haskey *in Population Trends*, Volume 91, Spring 1998 and subsequent years
Journal of the American Medicine Association, a study by a team led by Dr Edward Laumann 11.02.199
Marriage & Divorce Statistics, HMSO (various)
National Survey of Sexual Attitudes and Lifestyles in England
Office for National Statistics, January 2012
Policy Studies Institute Report 3 November 1998
Rowntree Foundation Report October 1998

Legislation

Abortion Act 1967
Command Paper 5629, July 2nd 1974
Contagious Diseases Act 1846
Criminal Justice (Terrorism & Conspiracy) Act 1988
Divorce Reform Act 1969
Family Planning Act 1967
Female Genital Mutilation Act 2003
Freedom of Information Act 2000
Married Women Property Act 1882
Matrimonial Causes Act 1857
Obscene Publications Act 1959
Prohibition of Female Circumcision Act 1985
Sexual Offences Act 1956, Section 6

www.ingramcontent.com/pod-product-compliance
Lightning Source LLC
Chambersburg PA
CBHW070633290526
45790CB00001B/86
9781484933596